ECHOES OF TRADITION

Exploring Girish Karnad's Theatrical Pilgrimage

Gitanjali Thapar

BlueRose ONE .com
Stories Matter
NewDelhi • London

BLUEROSE PUBLISHERS
India | U.K.

BlueRose ONE
Stories Matter
NewDelhi • London

For permissions requests or inquiries regarding this publication, please contact:

BLUEROSE PUBLISHERS
www.BlueRoseONE.com
info@bluerosepublishers.com
+91 8882 898 898
+4407342408967

ISBN: 978-93-6261-172-7

Cover Design: Sadhna Kumari
Typesetting: Pooja Sharma

First Edition: June 2024

Acknowledgements

Writing a book is a journey that demands patience, encouragement, and unwavering support. I am deeply grateful to the multitude of individuals who accompanied me through every step of this endeavour, since conception to completion. My heartfelt appreciation goes out to my family, whose steadfast encouragement sustained me through the arduous process of writing, editing, and formatting the manuscript. I am particularly indebted to Professor (Dr)Girija Sharma, former Dean of Studies, Himachal Pradesh University, Shimla whose unwavering belief in my abilities spurred me onward. Additionally, I extend my sincere gratitude to Professor (Dr) Sanjay Sindhu, Dean and Chairman, Faculty of Law, Himachal Pradesh University, Shimla for his invaluable guidance and insights, which significantly enriched the content of the book and imbued it with depth and meaning.

I feel extremely elated by the honourable Justice C.B Barowalia, Lokayukta, State of Himachal Pradesh, who graciously penned the foreword for my first book, adding prestige to its spirit and pages. Furthermore, I wish to express my thanks to my alma mater(s), St. Bedes College Shimla, and UILS, Ava Lodge Campus, Himachal Pradesh University, Shimla for providing me with a nurturing, conducive environment and equipping me with the skills necessary to pursue a career in teaching and in writing.

Their support has been instrumental in shaping my journey as an author. I am profoundly thankful to the Almighty for the blessings, and the divine grace that has illuminated my path throughout the endeavour of publishing this book.

Preface

India drama is embedded in the structural periphery of myths, folklores and legends. The legacy of culture and tradition has always inspired and fascinated various dramatists and theater artists. Typically set in the timeless, supernatural and mythological world of divine celestial beings, the gods and the goddesses, the Indian plays are enriched with theatrical nuances, which are to be deciphered and decoded in the contextual mode.

Our cultural roots have a strong hold on myths and legends as the fundamental element of human existence. The pages that follow exhibit the Indian aesthetics as woven in the plays of Girish Karnad in his major plays. The hybrid theatre pioneered by Girish Karnad and his contemporaries in the 19th century, presented a rich amalgam of tradition and culture. The inherent character of the roots movements is interfused with the modern Indian theatre. Recapitulating modern Indian theatre's struggle to liberate itself from the western realistic theatre the narratives acquire a distinct Indian flavor. Rooted in the rich cultural and theatrical sensibility the book presents the indigenous and the contemporary aesthetics making it relevant to the absurdity of the present day world.

JUSTICE C. B BAROWALIA
Lokayuta, Himachal Pradesh

Pines Grove
Shimla-171 002

Foreword

Preserving Indian ethos and cultural dimensions can significantly contribute in escalating harmony in the Indian society. The present book "Echoes of Tradition: Exploring Girish Karnad's Theatrical Pilgrimage" by Dr. Gitanjali Thapar, delves into a rich and thought provoking world of Girish Karnad's literary work exploring his iconic plays. The writer meticulously analyzed and unravel the intricate narratives, shedding light on unique perspectives, thematic concerns and artistic vision. The book is an amalgamation of Indian theatre and modern sensibility. Dr. Gitanjali has deeply gone into the cultural aspect of the work of Shri Girish Karnad's and highlighted the modern day impact with relation to the literary work. The writer has also beautifully depicted the mythological stories in her work.

I congratulate the author, Dr. Gitanjali Thapar for the publication of this book which resonates with timeless traditions and beliefs establishing a connection between the past and the present. I appreciate the work done by Dr. Gitanjali Thapar and hope that this will lead to happiness in the society.

Date: 02-04-2024

Justice C.B. Barowalia,
Lokayukta, Himachal Pradesh,

All the world's a stage,

And all the men and women merely players;

They have their exits and their entrances;

William Shakespeare

Contents

Chapter -1
Introduction

The Indian drama has undergone momentous transformation since its inception. While it flourishes in its new form it has also shown a tendency of revisiting its classical origins. Girish Karnad, being a leading playwright of the contemporary times, represents generation of playwrights, who have commendably resolved the conflict between modernity and tradition. These playwrights knew that they were faced with the huge task of liberating drama from its subjugation to colonial models. These playwrights, however, knew that it would not be wise to altogether dump the western dramaturgy. Therefore, while they decolonized the contemporary drama, they also worked towards finding an alternative modernity. Girish Karnad himself sums up the social and historical context of the contemporary drama:

My generation was the first to come of age after India became independent of British rule. It therefore had to face a situation in which tensions implicit until then had come out in the open and demanded to be resolved without apologia or self-justification: tensions between the attractions of Western modes of thought and our own traditions, and finally between the various visions of the future that opened up once the common cause of political freedom was achieved. This is the historical context that gave rise to my plays and those of my contemporaries. (Karnad, Three Plays, 1)

Modern Indian playwrights turned to a genre that was culture-specific, while being modern at the same time. It marks a return to the 'folk theatre' that had been completely sidelined during the colonial rule. For this reason, the emphasis was shifted more to performance while text-based western dramaturgy took a back seat. The dramatists looked for models in their cultural past. The scholars and playwrights began to look up to authoritative texts on Indian theatrical traditions for inspiration. Natyashstra, which is a universally accepted treatise on theatre, was published in the Gaekward Oriental series in 1926. This was the first critical edition edited by M. Ramakrishna Kavi. What came to be called the 'Theatre of Roots' was inspired not only by the folk theatre but also by the principles of the *Natyashastra.*

The *Natyashashtra* is a treatise on dramaturgy written in Sanskrit language. The name consists of two Sanskrit words 'Natya', meaning theatre, scenic action or more specifically drama, and 'Sastra', the term accepted in the Indian theatre tradition for holy writ dedicated to a particular field of knowledge. The book has a story about the birth of drama, which like all theories of origin needs to be decoded. The mode of presentation is one of dialogue between Bharata and the sages. It makes an inquiry into the nature of drama that unfolds the origin theory and technique of drama and theatre with all its components of speech, word, body-language, gesture, costuming, décor and the moods.

It is believed that the legendry author of the *Natyashashtra*, the Bharata Muni received his knowledge of dramatic art from none other than God Brahma, Bharata asserted that Brahma, the creator of this world also created drama and thus its origin cannot be questioned.

The *Natyashashtra* is one of the world's earliest treaties on theatre. Its first chapter tells the story of the birth of Drama. The legend has it that when the world was sunk in moral depravity and people had become slaves to irrational passions, new means had to be found which could uplift humanity. So Brahma the creator, combined elements from the four Vedas to form a fifth text, the Veda of performance. Since the gods were not capable of the discipline of drama, the new Veda was passed on to Bharata, a human being, who with the help of his hundred sons, and some celestial dancers sent by Brahma, staged the first play.

The first play dealt with the history of the conflict between the gods and the demons and celebrated the ultimate victory of the gods. The production delighted the gods and the humans, but the demons in the audience were deeply offended. Therefore, they used their supernatural powers and disrupted the performance by paralyzing the speech, movements and memory of the actors. The gods in turn attacked the demons and killed many of them. Brahma, the creator, approached the demons and explained that drama is the representation of the state of the three worlds. It incorporates the ethical goals of life-- the spiritual, the secular and the sensuous, as also its joys and sorrows. There is no wisdom, no art, no emotion which is not found in it.

The myth condemns the demons, as they had failed to comprehend the true nature of theatre. Thus, Brahma's discourse on theatre becomes the essence of the myth. The creator Brahama himself, along with other gods, celestial nymphs and trained actors, was involved in the project. The result should have been a roaring success. However, it was a disaster. The myth points to an essential characteristic of theatre that every performance, however carefully devised, carries within itself the risk of failure, of disruption and therefore, of violence. This age old myth also points out that the playwright, the performers and the audience form a continuum, but one which will always be unstable and therefore potentially explosive.

Brahma created drama so that the knowledge of the Vedas becomes accessible to all. He combined the four essential elements of theatre-'pathya', 'gana', 'abhinaya' and 'rasa' with the Vedic rituals. He established the sanctity and efficacy of 'natya' as the fifth Veda. The *Natyashastra* also provides us with a reliable historical picture of the correlation between ritual and drama, as the Indian drama originated from the religious rituals of the Vedas. According to the *Natyashastra,* the connection between rites, rituals and drama is that of mutual conditioning. The Sanskrit drama did not succeed to the rite. Neither did it originate out of the rite, but evolved parallel to it as part and parcel of the ritual ceremony.

The main object of the *Natyashastra* is to prescribe what should be shown and what should not be shown in a drama. What one hears and what one sees must be good, decent, decorous, pleasing, elevating and instructive. What is to be shown is the way of the world, 'lok-charita', and the doings of men, so that the audience gets education and guidance. According to Bharata, drama is the imitiation of men and their doings, 'loke-writa', 'anukarana'. The actions have to be presented on the stage, so drama is called in Sanskrit by the generic term 'roopaka' that which gives form. All the media of expression employed by an individual such as speech, gestures, movements and intonation, must be employed in a dramatic performance. The *Natyashastra* elaborately explains how language is formed and how sounds are produced and intonations employed to convey various shades of meaning.

The *Natyashastra* also prescribes the entire structure of a play from beginning to end. The play begins with poorvarang, 'a prologue' in which various deities are worshipped and which also includes dance and music to make the show more entertaining.

The theatre of roots follows many of the concepts and features as laid down by Bharata. Many playwrights use the technicalities as prescribed by Bharata, for example beginning a play with poorvarang, or 'a prologue', a common feature of western drama as well. The 'Sutradhara', that is, the holder of strings, begins the play in accordance with the rules laid down by Bharata. Karnad's *Hayavadana* opens with the address of the 'Sutradhara'.

Apart from these facts about the origin of drama, it can be said that Indian drama could not have come into its own without the availability of the highly developed mythological structure of the *Ramayana* and the *Mahabharata*. Besides all these influences, it can be assumed that the theatrical elements formed in the Vedic, ritualistic and mythological system served as the starting point for the ancient Indian drama.

Hindu religious literature was produced in successive periods of history and can be divided into different categories. The earliest was the Vedic period, assumed to be between 2500 BC and 600 BC. Four *Vedas: Rig, Yajur, Sama and Atharva* were composed by scholars whose identity remains unknown except for the fact that they must have been of the Aryan race. The oldest and the most important of the Vedas is the *Rig Veda,* which is a sizeable compilation of hymns. The *Rig Veda* has worldwide significance, uniqueness and irreparability. The *Rig Veda* is one of the pillars of knowledge on which the superstructure of Asian culture is built. In a rare honor, thirty *Rig Veda* manuscripts dating from 1800 to 1500 BC were included in Unesco's Memory of the World Register, a compendium of documentary heritage of exceptional value, in the year 2007.

The Vedas raise the level of Indian poetry to the metric level, and the *Upanishads* provide an imaginative reconstruction of Vedic hymns' experience. Max Muller rated the *Upanishads* as decidedly the chief canonical texts of the Indian poetic tradition. The Vedic religion consisted of a very developed mythology. Its pantheon lacked an absolute sovereign and distributed gods according to the regions occupied by them. Vedic mythology is concerned with the nature-myths and the functional deities, whose original function can be deduced from the etymology of their names. The *Vedas* offer in an embryonic state a majority of characteristics which developed with the passage of time.

The second period can be referred to as the epic (or Puranic) period. It was during this period, between 600 BC and AD 200 that the great epics of Hinduism the *Mahabharata* and the *Ramayana* were composed. The *Mahabharata* is the older and the more voluminous of the two epics; it is, in fact, the longest religious epic of the world, running into as many as 2009 chapters. The *Mahabharata* is full of stories within stories, which have been retold, rewritten and reinterpreted over the centuries, each conveying some moral lesson. All the Vedic mythology, all the existing folklore, the entire legendary literature and even the various forms of religion and schools of philosophy are described in the *Mahabharata*.

The period also saw the flowering of Hindu philosophical thought to its fullness. Commentaries on the Vedas, known as the *Upanishads* were written. The *Upanishads* were about two hundred in number. The *Bhagvad Gita*, considered as a great piece of Hindu religious writing, is the culmination of the teaching of the *Vedas* and the *Upanishads*. It is 'the most exalted of India's religious poems.' The Gita has inspired much religious and secular writing. The *Bhagvad Gita* is the sixteenth chapter in the epic of the *Mahabharata. The Bhagvad Gita* could be taken as the best representation of the Upanishad philosophy — a piece of literature that in T.S. Eliot's words is the greatest poem of the world, second only to Dante's *Divine Commedia*. It has symbolic, archetypal, metaphorical and moral values. Attempts have been made to read it while deconstructing it. One can also find strains of existentialism in the text.

It is this vast canvas of themes, on which the playwrights of the Theater of Roots movement based their plays. These playwrights, rooted in the Indian traditional culture, explored every possible area of interest being aroused by these literary canons. The roots movement strengthened the point that these epics contain the truth of human existence. *The Vedas*, the *Puranas* and the *Upanishads* are of eternal value to the Indian literary tradition.

The text has been seen as a ritual in the Indian tradition. The whole Vedic culture is based upon yajanas, or oblations offered to the fire. The fire germinates for us the seeds; seeds sprout and grow into trees and this cycle goes on in an eternal continuum. That is what the puranic models of toxicology explains. Most of the *Purans* have a cyclic structure with tales of creation and destruction that go on renewing themselves. Nature plays a key role in such cycles and Krishna the cow boy steals the show. "The centre and the periphery try to dominate each other with victory to both and defeat to none " (Sheel Singh, 27).

After the decline of classical Sanskrit drama, it was the *Charanas*, caste-professionals who substituted a form of dance drama in place of written plays. The dance-drama gained popularity, which encouraged the kings to write new compositions to patronize the Nati class.

The revival of *Shaivisim* and *Vashnavism* and *Bhakti* cult led to the emergence of the language of the people, as the medium which gained momentum and their religious revival led to the construction of a number of temples by kings. A numbers of plays were written and performed during these days. Thus, the *Charanas,* the kings and the saints can be said to have laid the foundations of modern Indian drama.

About the 14th century, a new form of dance-drama came into being which came to be known as 'Kalakshepa' or 'Harikatha'. 'Harikatha' is a one-man show. There is no stage, no scenes and no make-up and it is often arranged in a temple-yard, where the entrance is free. The themes were culled from the *Bhagavata*, *Mahabharata* or from the epic *Ramayana*. Various deities are praised in the beginning and the Harikatha artist like the Sutradhar of a play introduces the characters to the audience and also informs the audience as to which part of the story he would be reciting and finally comes to the story.

This Sutradhar is well acquainted with mythological stories. With the help of gestures and voice modulations, he creates different characters. He improvises the dialogue, quotes from the scholarly Sanskrit texts and explains their meaning with apt illustrations from contemporary experiences.

Harikatha recitation came to be known as a means of achieving 'punya' (merit). The *Bhakti* doctrine on the one hand and the Brahmin *Harikatha* artists on the other propagated this belief. The *Charana* and the artists influenced the beginning of modern Indian drama in the different linguistic regions of India. The essential contents, however, remain the same everywhere. The themes from the *Bhagvata* or sometimes heroic tradition, dance and music were incorporated in their renderings with all the technicalities of Sanskrit drama.

The elements that go into the making folk-drama, were handed over to the folk-stage by the Bhakti-school of drama. It also strengthened the direct contact between the audience and the actors. The *Charana*, the *Harikatha* artists and the Sutradhar were also linked together. The foundation of the folk-stage of India was laid on this well crafted structure.

The *Natyashastra* also recognises the existence of the folk stage. As mentioned earlier, Bharata composed his *Natyashastra*, to recognise the ten forms (das rupaka) of drama and to prescribe the do's and don't of the stage. The folk-stage exploited the legends of bravery of the heroes of *the Mahabharata* and the noble life of Rama. These two epics also provided the main source for the themes of folk-plays.

The drama and theatre in India suffered a complete blackout for a period of five or six centuries. This period of eclipse is also commonly referred to as the Dark Age in the Indian dramatic history. The curtain rises again in the middle of the eighteenth century. Form the decline of Sanskrit drama to the rise of the modern drama the classical drama existed in some form or the other in the first century A.D. with sporadic and artificial revivals taking place throughout the subsequent centuries.

What emerged as the modern Indian drama, though rooted in the Sanskrit drama for technique and theme, was influenced by the western drama as well. Many playwrights of the pre-independence periods followed the tradition of Elizabethan drama in general and of Shakespeare in particular.

It took a century and a quarter for Indian drama in English to reach respectability. In 1831 the first Indian English play was written by Krishan Mohan Banerji, The *Persecuted or Dramatic Scenes of the Present State of Hindoo Society in Calcutta.* It is a social play which presents the conflict between Indian orthodoxy and the new ideas which came from the west. It exposes the hypocrisy of the affluent in Hindu society and also refers to the historic theme of East-West encounter.

Rabindranath Tagore, Sri Aurobindo, H.N. Chattopadhytaya, T.P. Kailasam are playwrights of considerable merit who made epoch making and abiding contribution to the development of Indian drama, towards the close of the last century.

Tagore was an ardent admirer of Kalidasa, Shakespeare and Ibsen. He modelled most of his plays on the five-act structure of Elizabethan drama. Poetic in temperament and outlook, Tagore reveled in the employment of imagery and symbolism in his plays. Deeply influenced by the classical Sanskrit literature, he had extensive knowledge of Indian epics, *Vedas* and *Upanishads*, which is reflected in many of his plays.

Sri Aurbindo's writings bear testimony of his profound knowledge of Eastern and Western thought. In his play *Perseus the Deliverer*, he uses the perseus myth to unfold the suffering and travails of the fighters engaged in the struggle for India's freedom. The theme of his play *Vasavadatta* is borrowed from Somadva's *Kathasritasagar*, one of the most popular Sanskrit classics.

In a similar vain, many other playwrights also used the Sanskrit classics and the epics *Ramayana* and *Mahabharata* in their plays. The mythology, folk legends, religious rituals and folk lores have, thus, been incorporated by the playwrights in drama over a period of time.

The early period of the resurgence of the Indian drama was, therefore, marked by a tendency to follow the rich tradition of the classical Sanskrit drama and the folk-theatre. This leaning among the playwrights however, shared a space with their fondness for the Elizabethan dramatic idiom. This was largely because of the availability of the British dramatic models and the awe these inspired among the educated Indians. Despite some serious efforts to return to their roots, the playwrights were still struggling to revive their classical heritage. In this connection G.P. Despande observes:

A search for authentic 'Indian Theatre has begun … This search had two distinct features. It postulated a comparable if not uniform 'Indian' theatre. It also postulated a notion of theatre which is civilization-specific. It would be a theatre of Indian forms which would be completely understandable; it would also be theatre of 'Indian timeless content' which is not easily understandable (Deshpande, x).

The present age has seen great works of art being written in various Indian languages. These works of great literary value and cultural centrality have made a great impact on the contemporary literary scene, emphasizing the need to make these available to people all over the country. Consequently, literature written in regional languages is being translated into English and other languages, thus establishing closer ties between different regions of India.

At the same time, some serious literature has been produced in English by the Indians in recent years. This literature is both an Indian literature and a variation of English literature. This body of writing has been designated as Indo-Anglian literature, which is used to denote original literary creation in the English language by Indians. Indo-English literature is also a term used to classify the literature consisting of translations by Indians from Indian literature into English.

A significant fallout of such vigorous literary activity is particularly visible in the field of drama, which is the most popular medium of entertainment. In this way, regional drama in India has slowly paved the way for a "national theatre" into which all streams of theatrical art came together. The major language theatre, such as Hindi, Bengali, Marathi and Kannada active all through the fluctuating years of regeneration and strengthening, led to the emergence of great playwrights in major Indian languages.

Among the pioneers of this new resurgence are Mohan Rakesh, Badal Sircar, Vijay Tendulkar and Girish Karnad among others. Their plays have been translated in other regional languages as well as in English. As such, they have succeeded in building a national theatre movement.

These playwrights presented a variety of themes in their plays and contributed significantly towards innovative style. Most of their plays were experiments of an intense and deeply felt emotion rather than superficial innovations. They infused a basic simplicity and naturalness coupled with a meaningful depth in their plays.

Karnad is also a part of the "theatre of roots" movement, which typifies search for an indigenous dramatic Idiom. Theatre of roots is one of the vibrant theatre movements in the recent history of Indian theatre, pioneered by Ratan Thiyam. Ratan Thiyam is one of the most important directors of contemporary Indian theatre, a distinction which he has achieved through his purposeful work. He comes from Manipur of the North Eastern states of India. During the late 60's and early 70's, Indian theatre experienced a period of re-awakening to its own traditional heritage. The theatre pandits were advocating a National theatre to be evolved from our own roots and rituals. The playwrights started to question the western sensibility, western style of production and its techniques. Ratan Thiyam answered this call with his powerful productions, real spectacles of movement, a renewed audio-visual sensibility with fresh native energy. It can be defined as the mixed dramatic idiom developed by certain post-independence playwrights and directors who modified certain aspects of traditional Indian genres to the modern proscenium stage. The rejection of proscenium stage was one part of the overall rejection of the western idiom in favour of a native one. Plot and characterization became secondary and the actor became more important than the character. Later it became a common feature of the individual doctrines of such stalwarts like K.N Panikar, Ratan Thiyam and Habib Tanvir to name a few.

The exponents of this movement rebelled against British-influenced drama, turning to their roots in folk and classical performances to create a modern theatre that would be genuinely Indian. As Erin B. Mee puts it: "Thus, the theatre of roots movement can be best understood as a way of decolonizing the theatre, as a politically driven search for an indigenous aesthetic and dramaturgy" (Mee, 2).She further adds that the goal of this movement is "to establish a modern universal, indigenous national theatre in India". A number of playwrights and directors turned to classical dance, religious ritual and other forms of popular entertainment along with Sanskrit aesthetic theory to see what dramaturgical structures, acting styles and staging techniques could be used to create an indigenous modern Indian theatre. "This impulse became known as the theatre of roots movement – a post-independence effort to decolonize the aesthetics of modern Indian theatre by challenging the visual practices, performer spectator relationships, dramaturgical structures and aesthetic goals of colonial performance" (Mee, Enacting, 5).

The theatre of roots movement was the first conscious effort to produce a body of work that synthesized modern European theatre and traditional Indian performance – creating a new, hybrid theatrical form. As director M.K. Raina, puts it "We are not going back to tradition… we are in the process of creating new thinking, new sensibilities, and therefore new forms. Perhaps the fusion of some of the traditional forms and contemporary struggles may give birth to vital new forms, representative of contemporary Indian reality" (136-8). This new theatrical form is not at all anti-modern but challenges "a cultural definitions of modernity that define modernity and modern theatre in and on western terms" (Mee, 5).

One of the important characteristics of the roots movement is that the directors and playwrights "complicate the linear narrative", incorporating "multiplicity of voices and multiple perspectives on a particular theme or story" (Mee, 6). The most renowned practitioners of this influential theatrical innovation are Kavalam Narayana Panikkar, Girish Karnad and Ratan Thiyam. Production is given prominence which gives an opportunity for "multivocality", for privileging voices other than just that of playwright (Mee, 6). Similarly, "vocal expression and physicality" (Mee, 6) serve a parallel means of communications providing information and commentary on the text. The commentary is conveyed through "physical movement, vocal gestures… music and non-verbal modes of expression" (Mee, 6) to communicate experiences. "This is an excellent example of the way the theatre of roots focuses on multisensory, multilayered and performance-driven events for an actively engaged audience" (Mee, 6).

There are two major aspects of the theatre of roots: "the impulses of the individual artist", which compel him to turn to the roots in traditional genres of performance. The traditional genres included techniques and aesthetics from the colonial theatre and the 'cultural dichotomy' thus formed, profoundly influenced the theatre of roots movement which developed as a response to colonial definitions of modern theatre. Girish Karnad in most of his, plays combines the Western dramaturgical structure with the modern theatrical tradition to which he could relate and express his ideas. Karnad uses myths in many of his plays to refer to the complexities of present age and apprehension of present age and apprehension about future. But he combines the Indian myths and stories with their Indian setting with western dramaturgy. Karnad has based many of his plays on myths and epics from India. But he combines them with western dramaturgy. Consequently, he succeeded in devising an indigenous dramatic structure. Habib Tanvir found the western dramatic idiom "inadequate for effectively projecting the social aspirations, way of life, cultural patterns and fundamental problems of contemporary India" (Mee, 7) Habib Tanvir also felt that two centuries of alien rule had annihilated India's cultural identity. So he called for "our own plays about our own problems in our own forms" (Mee, 7). Habib Tanvir, Vijay Tendulkar, Vijaya Mehta, Satish Alekar, Neelam Man Singh Chowdhry, Arjun Raina and Maya Krishna Rao are among the pioneers of modern drama to use elements of popular performance in their productions. They believed that the theatre forms borrowed from the west were not sufficient to efficaciously portray the hopes, dreams, anxieties and cultural configurations of contemporary Indian society.

Ratan Thiyam graduated from the National School of Drama (NSD) in Delhi in 1974 and acquired knowledge about the Western theatre. When he returned to Manipur to work he realized that his western training came in the way of communicating with his audience. Alongwith other playwrights, he strove to create a theatre which would involve community, because theatre, afterall, is a collective experience. The prominent Malayalam – language playwright G. Sankara Pillai spearheaded the movement to formulate the principles of 'Theatre of Roots'. Actors, theatre critics and playwrights got together and organized workshops to work for a new drama culture based on the performing arts of Kerala. C.N. Sreekantan Nair "coined the term *thanathunatakavedi* in the 1960s to describe the new theatre. Thanathu means 'one's own'; nataka translates as 'drama', 'story' or 'play', and vedi is 'stage' – so *thanathunatakavedi* means 'one's own theatre'" (Mee, 8). Pillai wanted Kerala's performing arts to be recognized as "modern theatre forms that reflected the aesthetics of these genres rather than the aesthetics of British theatre" (Mee, 8). The idea of *thanathunatakavedi* was adopted by Panikkar "in opposition to Western text-based naturalism" as a response to what he has called the 'onslaught of alien influences on our aesthetic sensibilities' (Mee, 9). Panikkar regarded it as "not just drama but drama culture" (Mee, 8).

Ngugi wa Thiong'o talks about the way colonialism not only controlled people's wealth but also "the mental universe of the colonized" (Ngugi, 16). Panikkar defines *thanathunatakavedi* as a process which 'is to be understood as the discovery of the self' through theatre (Mee, 9). The major difference between Western and Indian theatre is that the western theatre has textual orientation and the Indian theatre is performance oriented. Many western avant-garde artists also scoffed at the text-based naturalistic western theatre. Many theatre artists wanted to dismantle the aesthetics of the western theatrical practices. As a result, serious efforts were made to turn to the aesthetics of Indian drama. In the year 1918 Dr. Suresh Awasthi coined the term 'theatre of roots' to describe modern Indian theatre's 'encounter with tradition' characterized as a 'liberation from Western realistic theatre' (Mee, 12). This theatre was expected to reflect the issues related to historical, political, social and cultural situation of the nation that was struggling to be independent.

After independence the Sangeet Natak Akademi (SNA) and the National Academy of Music, Dance and Drama came into being in Delhi. Through a series of festivals produced by the Akademi between 1984 and 1991, a group of artists spread across the nation and used traditional performance in the making of their modern theatre. These artists developed 'a theatre idiom indigenous in character, inspired by the folk/traditional theatre of the country' (Mee, 11). As Dharwadker points out, "the quest [was] not so much for a "national theatre" as for a significant theatre *in* and *of* the nation, linked intra-nationally by complex commonalities and mutual self-differentiations" (Dharwadkder, 24). The SNA promoted an indigenous theatrical idiom and a community of theatre lovers, artists and playwrights by making regional drama accessible to readers and playgoers. The roots movement thus emerged as the most powerful post-independence theatrical movement in India.

Erin B. Mee refers to Partha Chatterjee who distinguishes between three stages of nationalist thought, which contributed towards the development of the theatre of roots.

The first stage, the moment of departure, recognizes an 'essential cultural difference between East and West' in which the West is thought to be superior in terms of its material culture, its science, its technology and its commitment to progress, while the East is thought to be 'superior in the spiritual aspects of culture'. The second stage, the moment of manoeuvre, 'consists in the historical consolidation of the "national" by decrying the "modern". In the case of the roots movement, traditional performance (including religious ritual and the non-technological aspects of performance practice) was defined and mobilized as that which represented 'Indian culture'. The final stage, the moment of arrival, occurs when the discourse is 'conducted in a single, consistent, unambiguous voice' at which point it 'succeeds in glossing over all earlier contradictions, divergences and differences' (Mee, 16).

Amal Allana, chairperson of the NSD in an interview (with Amrith Lal of *The Times of India*) reveals that National theatre has meaning, "as the local has become the global. Boundaries have been dissolving at such a fast rate that describing any theatre …, as a national theatre has become extremely difficult".(Lal , *The Times of India*)

Allana refers to India as a country, which is actually a continent with a rich theatrical legacy …. and aesthetics [of its own]". She further remarks that there was a time when an attempt was made to create a national culture during India's freedom struggle and in the Nehruvian era "when people believed in an Indian or utopian monolith. But this was short-lived because it was neither relevant nor possible". She stresses that "the issue today is to decentralize everything and rediscover the path that we have in part lost sight of in the past twenty years".

India's independence in 1947 sparked a movement to return to more traditional practices, and Mee considers Girish Karnad as one of the most pivotal figures of the Theatre of Roots. His play *Hayavadana*, begins with a ritual offering; Karnad invites the audience to see the play both as a Western audience would and as a traditional Indian work at the same time – a "double viewing" in which the spectator sees simultaneous realities at once.

Son of Raghunath, and Kasibai, Karnad was born in Matheran, a small town near Mumbai in Maharashtra on May 19, 1938. Though his mother tongue is Kannada, he had his initial schooling in Marathi. Most of Karnad's plays were originally written in Kannada. Many of them have been translated into other languages and English. The English translations of his plays are his own. They have brought him international acclaim as a pre-eminent contemporary playwright.

He passed through a rewarding and enriching academic career from graduation to Doctor of Letters. After graduating from Karnataka University in 1958, Karnad moved to Bombay for further studies. He received the prestigious Rhodes scholarship and went to England for Master's degree.

During his stay at Magadalen College, Oxford, Karnad found himself getting deeply interested in art and culture. On his return to India in 1963, he joined the Oxford University Press, Madras. This offered him an opportunity to get exposed to various kinds of writings in India and elsewhere. Such exposure left an indelible mark on his creative genius.

During his formative years in a small village in Karnataka, Karnad had the first hand experience of the indigenous folk-theatre. The dramatic performances made a lasting impression on his mind. Karnad acknowledges the contribution of the Natak Mandalis and says:

It may have something to do with the year that in the small town of Sirsi... Natak 'companies, would come, set up a stage, present a few plays… I loved going to see them and the magic has stayed with me. (Karnad, Three Plays, Vol.1, vi)

It was his parent's fondness for plays and his own interest in them that started shaping him into a successful dramatist from his early years. It was his great desire to be a poet but he realized in his early twenties that his true vocation was to be a dramatist. As a young man studying in the provincial Karnataka College in Dharwar he had one burning ambition—to go to England and write poetry in English. "I wanted to be internationally famous like Shakespeare and T.S. Eliot", he confesses.

As observed already, Karnad stayed in England on a Rhodes scholarship. During that period he was attracted by great authors such as Giradoux, Anouilh, Camus and Sarte in his search for new forms of drama. But Indian mythology and epics still fascinated him a great deal. So he found himself irresistibly drawn towards them. His reworking of myths, Puranic, historical and literary, puts him in the same category as Kailasam and Rangacharya as much as to those European dramatists who recreate their myths.

In 1974, he received an important assignment and was appointed the Director of Film and Television Institute of India, Pune. In 1987, he went to U.S.A. as Fulbright Scholar-in-Residence at the Department of South Asian Languages and Civilizations, University of Chicago. From 1988 to 1993, he served as Chairman of the Sangeet Natak Academy, New Delhi. In 1994, he was awarded Doctor of Letters degree by the Karnataka University, Dharwad. He was awarded the Padma Bhushan in 1992 and the Jnanpith award, the country's highest literary recognition for his contributions to modern Indian drama.

Karnad has acted, directed and scripted a numbers of films and documentaries, which have won awards; including the award-winning movie *Samskara.* His films have been shown at film festivals all over the world. Karnad has also acted in several Hindi and Kannada feature films, for well known directors such as Satyajit Ray, Mrinal Sen and Shyam Benegal. He made his mark in films like "Manthan", "Godhuli" and "Ratandeep", and won the Best Actor Award for his performance in "Swami". Still he makes a starting revelation. "I never wanted to be an actor". His recent film where he is cast as an actor is *Life Goes On*, a Stormglass production, UK. After a hiatus, Karnad has returned to the screen in Girish Acharya's film "Brides Wanted' which has stimulated him to write a contemporary play "The Wedding Album" based on a wedding in a middle class family.

Karnad's works include *Yayati* (1961), *Tughlaq* (1964), *Hayavadana* (1971), *Hittina Hunja* (1980), *Naga Mandala: Play with a Cobra* (1988), *Agni Mattu Male (The Fire and the Rain)* (1995), *the Dreams of Tipu Sultan, Bali: The Sacrifice* (2004), *Taledanda. Broken Images and Flowers* are two monologues published in the year 2005.His most recent play is *The Wedding Album*, (2009).

Karnad's drama is all about re-presenting the known and the familiar in a novel manner. Using folktales, mythological and historical legends he "weaves together timeless truths about human life and emotions contained in ancient Indian epics, legends and Upanishads" (Gupta, 249). As Karnad experiments boldly with technique, his plays forge a bond between the past and the present. He obviously refers to the past while delving deep into the world of myths and folklore. But the spirit of his drama is unmistakably modern. He not only links the past with the present but also the grandeur and mobility of the epics like the *Mahabharata* and *Ramayana* with the simplicity and charm of folk imagination. Thus, mingling the epic and the folk strains, his drama acquires a universal appeal and imaginative richness.

Karnad's ingenuity and artistic skill consists in the way he examines the tales he incorporates in his drama, from his own point of view along with their historical mythic perspective. The subject is then developed by him "in the crucible of his own imagination and personal experiences, and [he] employs them as a medium to communicate his own independent and original feelings, thoughts and interpretations."(Chatterji,1)

Although rooted in Indian mythology and history, his plays convey a strong and unmistakable affinity for the western philosophical sensibility as well. The existentialist crisis of modern man is conveyed through strong individuals who are torn by intense psychological and philosophical battle raging within their mind.

Based on his serious explorations of folklore, mythology and history, the subjects of his plays reflect the problems and challenges of contemporary life, and endeavour to forge a link between the past and the present. 'Karnad has been accused of escaping into the past", says Lakshmi Chandra-Shekhar and academic and an active figure in Kannada theatre."But the use of mythology in most modern literature validates individual experience and universalizes it. And I think Karnad has been able to do that"(Dass,71)

Thematically, Karnad offers a rich variety of plays which refer to myths. His first play *Yayati* is based on an episode in the *Mahabharata*. The play revolves around the legendary *Yayati*, one of the ancestors of the Pandavas, Shukracharya and Puri. Thus, Karnad combines the myth of Yayati with the characters of *Mahabharata* and examines the moments of crisis and dilemma which are at the core of the play. The play *Yayati* which is a self-consciously existentialist drama on the theme of responsibility shows the influence of Camus and Satre as well.

Karnad's fusion of the Indian and the Western theatrical tradition is reflected in the story of *The Transposed Heads* in *Hayavadana*. The mind versus the body debate from Thomas Mann's *Transposed Heads* in *Hayavadana* echoes the Cartesian concept of duality. The play is a 'riddling philosophical thriller in which Karnad "problematises the issues of personal identity"(Chatterji,1) The theme of incompleteness runs throughout the play and to highlight this aspect, Karnad puts into use the Indian myths, associated with Lord Ganesha presenting them as archetypes. The transposition of the heads constitutes the main crux of the play, which results in a confusion of identities, revealing the essential ambiguity of human nature. In *Hayavadna* , Karnad blends mythological and the folk legends with the theme of universal quest for perfection and completeness. The Ganesha myth is interfused with the myth of Hayavadana, the man with the head of a horse. The motif of transposed heads is further extended to the story of Kapila and Devdatta. The multilayered structure of the play points towards a single meaning, that is, the eternal search for perfection and completeness.

Karnad has always taken a leading part in movements and crusades concerning social and cultural issues of India. In the recent years, he has been a bitter critic of religious fundamentalism in India. In his play *Tale-Danda*, Karnad tries to explore the evil effects of social deformity at cultural, social and psychological levels. In this play, Karnad deals with the political situation of a turbulent state. The play takes up the issue of reform movement and the rise of Virshavism, a radical protest movement in 12th century Karnataka to explicitly deal with the influence of the larger social and intellectual milieu on individual action.

Karnad foregrounds the social context of individual conflict, something that is further developed in *Agni Mattu Male (The Fire and the Rain)*, his most popular play. Karnad here deals with the traditional controversy between asceticism and rituals. The source of the play comes from the *Mahabharata.* It is an obscure story, with a play within a play, which centres around a fire sacrifice to bring rain. Karnad's play is a masterpiece mapping conflicting human emotions. It is an excellent combination of human, metaphysical and supernatural elements.

The Fire and the Rain employs several myths and legends, each having a standpoint of its own. All these viewpoints, however, refer to the central story. Karnad's disillusionment with dead and worn-out traditions is clearly discernible in the play. It is an outright condemnation of the dogma and hypocrisy associated with the orders of religion. Another point driven home through mythic references is the possibility of the annihilation of the cosmos itself, if human vices rampant in society go unchecked.

In *Bali The Sacrifice*, Karnad strengthens the belief that indulging in any kind of violence, however minor or accidental, meant forfeiting one's moral status as a human being. Based on his serious explorations of folklore, mythology and history, his plays reflect the problems and challenges of contemporary life and endeavour to forge a link between the past and the present.

Karnad turns away from the 'classical' traditions as his source to local Kannada folk-tales in *Naga-Mandala*. Here he combines two tales, the central one focusing on the snake-lover motif, "while the frame story explores the notion of stories having a life independent of their narrators, derived from oral traditions"(Chatterji,3). Karnad draws heavily on the legend of the supposed powers of the Naga to transform itself into any shape. The significance of the play, however, extends beyond the surface charm and simplicity of the tale of a serpent. What is fore-grounded is the essential reality associated with the "experience of men and women in the psychologically transitory phase" (Gupta, 250) of growth into selfhood. The serpent myth is also used to highlight the essentially feministic bias of the play.

The play *Tughlaq*, of the sixties, presents a "rich and complex symbolism and also reflects the mood of disillusionment which followed the Nehru era of idealism in the country. *Tughlaq's* thematic concerns have a universal significance. Karnad here critically explores the psychic structure of the characters and brings to the fore the fundamental human motives with a distinctive, masterly control. The play is more than a political allegory and the treatment of the theme is not entirely historical. The dualism of the man and the hero in *Tughlaq* is the source of the entire tragedy. The play presents Muhammad-Bin-Tughlaq, the enigmatic character, who keeps on changing his roles. The focus is on the psychological implication of the theme of human power in respect of a self-righteous idealist, who wants to exercise absolute power over his subjects. Karnad's Tughlaq has been compared by critics to Camus *Caligula*, for both the plays present a tyrant using his power absolutely and indulging in senseless cruelty. There are many references to acting, theatre, and performance in *Tughlaq.* The play highlights one of the fundamental concepts of theatre, that theatre is an illusion, a fleeting shadow, a vision and a dream-like experience.

Karnad's monologue *'Broken Images'* takes sustenance from the images of the 'now'. It explores the facets of the urban Indian society with its fascination for technology. In an interview Karsnad calls it "a technically intricate play" (Konkani,1). He further adds that the "in a sense, [the play] is a comment on the relationship between theatre and T.V. the real and the virtual." The Kannada version is called *Odakalu Bimba.* It is a story about a woman professor in English literature Manjula Naik who writes in Kannada and is being interviewed on TV after she has won accolades for her literary work in English. As the interview ends she gets up to go but her image on the screen wants to stay on. It wants to talk to her; she gets scared but then starts talking. The play is essentially a discussion between the woman and her image. The monologue foreshadows Karnad's own experience as a playwright who has faced broad criticism in Karnataka for being 'westernized' as he writes in English.

Karnad, pointing to the literary scene in India today says that writers in English are rewarded with acclaim, recognition and money while regional writers have to fight hard for all o these. "It's money and public recognition that English brings, that itself is a point of envy", explains Karnad. And that is the underlying theme of this play; envy as part of the human condition that manifests itself in today's globalised world, and the 'politics' of writing as Karnad refers to the literary scenes today. Manjula Nayak's talk on TV defending her choice of language in a talk she gives on a television channel sounds suspiciously like a repartee from Karnad to his detractors. Nayak's alter ego on a television screen is an innovative method of including modern technology in drama. Another interesting aspect of the play is the subsequent dramatic unfolding of Nayak's innermost motives and actions from the "private self" of the public image that continues to both intrigue and shock. This play is different from the other plays of Karnad, that revolve around mythology and folklore. The sense of contemporaneity sets it apart from the other "roots" plays, but incorporates cultural image of present day India. For this reason, it marks an important phase in Karnad's writing. Karnad's *Wedding Album* is a family drama set in a middle-class family where twenty two years old Vidula is looking forward to her arranged marriage, with an NRI in the US. The play has a typical Indian flavor. The play also brings up the issue of how some rituals are broken by the present generation in today's "technologically savvy India".

Flowers is based on a folk-tale from Chitradurga region in Karnataka. In this play Karnad reverts to the world of folklore and takes up the legend of Veeranna. The legend was used by T.R. Subbanna in his novel *Hamsageethe* (Swan Song). Karnad 'recasts the legend as a conflict between religious devotion and erotic love, undergirded by the priest's guilt at his daily betrayal of his wife' (Karnad, Vol. 2).

Girish Karnad has a keen sense of utilizing essential theatricality for appropriate effect. He is a good theatre maker and a good writer and his work uses a whole range of theatrical form, engages with central social and political issues of recent and contemporary Indian life.

Karnad's ability to universalize the individual and social predicament of human beings through the medium of drama has given his works a wide appeal. As already noted his works have been translated into several Indian languages and staged by eminent directors such as E. Alkazi, Satyadev Dubey, B.V. Karnath, Alyque Padamsee, Vijay Mehta, Shyammanand Jalan and Amal Allana. They have also been translated and performed for audiences abroad. As A.K. Sinha puts it:

In all his plays—be the theme mythical, historical or legendary, Karnad's approach is modern and he uses the conventions and motifs of folk art, like masks and curtains to project a world of intensities, uncertainties and unpredictable denouements (Sinha, 24).

Karnad believes that the energy of folk theatre comes from the fact that although it serves to uphold traditional values, it also has the means of questioning these values. V.Rangan in his article "Myth and Romance in *Naga-Mandala* or their Subversion" attaches a label to the interplay of folk imagination and folk play in the plays of Karnad and remarks:

Folk imagination is at once mythopoeia and magical. In the folk mind, one subsumes the other. Folk belief, besides being naïve, has a touch of poetry about it which works towards a psychic adjustment. All folklore is religious, often based on animism because the primitive imagination extends its vision from the natural, in which it is steeped and with which it is saturated, to the supernatural, which to the folk mind is only an extension of the former (Rangan, 199).

In affinity with the Brechtian theatre, Karnad's theatre is a theatre with a purpose. He does not advocate a theatre by which the spectators become emotionally involved in a play. Therefore, like Bertolt Brecht, Karnad works for the 'alienation effect' making the stage devices visible, making announcements and allowing the narrators directly talk to the audience. A fine example of this can be seen in *Hayavadana,* where Bhagvata speaks to the audiences in the course of the play and keeps them updating about the happenings, while reviewing each and every situation in the play.

In the drama of Girish Karnad, myth is not merely a ritual or a structural device. It is a means of exploring a modern outcome of a traditional situation. Karnad in his plays tries to establish a 'dialectical relationship between tradition and modernity'(Ravindran, India Today), which is also a central theme in contemporary Indian society and literature. Karnad's drama, therefore, has a distinct contemporary flavour. He strives to give a new meaning to the past, examining it in the context of the disturbing scenario of the present. In his work there exists a harmonious relationship between his versatility as a true artist and his ingenious handling of mythic and the folk material. By reverting to the rich mythic and folkloric Indian culture, he articulates his concerns in consistently engaging 'language of total performativity' (Chatterji, The Hindu).

Karnad does not employ the myths in their entirety. He picks up threads of legends and folk tales that he finds useful. He adds to these tales his imagination to construct the plots. The technique of fringing together myths, legends and folk narratives is his forte. He combines the literary and the folk elements with an unparalleled skill.

The principle involved in projecting myths in literature is the preservation of tradition. According to Alan W. Watt 'myth is to be defined as a complex of stories-some no doubt fact and some fantasy—which for various reasons human beings regard as demonstrations of the inner meaning of the universe and of human life(Gurine,16). Karnad has a keen sense of utilizing essentially theatrical qualities for appropriate effect. He uses a variety of literary devices such as the masks, chorus, music and the mixing of the human and the non-human worlds to enrich the literariness of the texts. All these conventions employed by him permit a simultaneous presentation of alternative points of view through mythic and folkloric traditions.

Northrop Frye, the most eminent of contemporary mythopoeic critics define myth as follows:

... in the history of civilization literature follows after a mythology. A myth is a simple and primitive effort of the imagination to identify the human with the non-human world, and its most typical result is a story about a god (Frye, 13).

Karnad seems to be doing what Frye has asserted. In his plays myth becomes a structural principle of story-telling and mythology inevitably begins to merge into literature (91).

Application of mythopoeic criticism is central to the study and analysis of Karnad's plays as it takes us far beyond the historical and aesthetic realms of literature. The mythopoeic approach s is used as a critical method which considers "literature as the ultimate embodiment of myth and ritual in the form of art". This methodology insists upon the fact that society and literature depend upon each other and approaches literature as a means of expressing human emotion and experience. A mythopoeic critic "sees the work holistically, as the manifestation of vitalizing, integrative forces arising from the depth of humankind's collective psyche" (Guerin, 167). Frye in *The Stubborn Structure* claims that:

Mythology as a whole provides a kind of diagram or blueprint of what literature as a whole is all about, an imaginative survey of the human situation from the beginning to the end, from the height to the depth, of what is imaginatively conceivable (102).

Myths have long been recognized as the structural organizing principle of a work of art. Besides imparting an organizational unity to the literary form, myths and legend also have the power to combine the alien and the inaccessible world of gods and the recognizable and accessible world of mortals.

The mythological approach to literature assumes that there is a collection of symbols, images, characters and motifs that are recognizable and evoke basically the same response in every work of art. This approach tries to surface out meanings by decoding the metaphorical and symbolic nuances in a work of art while still remaining humanistically connected with its aesthetic appeal.

Mythological themes are consciously employed in literature to bring out certain ideas which can be expressed through the projection of myths. Mythopoeic critics use the similarities and differences to argue and discover the underlying themes and hidden meanings of a myth. In a similar vein, plays are written, putting forward certain themes imbued with mythological symbols motifs and legends. Mythology encompasses a wide range of subject matter for a dramatist as well and gives a wider scope to construct a work of literature. Myths therefore become the symbolic projections of human aspirations, hopes, fears and values.

The pre-modern theories interpret myths on account of historical events. Various distortions occur because of the telling and re-telling of many myths. During the second half of the nineteenth century attempts were made to interpret myth scientifically. E.B. Taylor interpreted myth as an attempt at a literal explanation for natural phenomena. He speculated that early man attributed souls to inanimate objects and tried to explain natural phenomena thereby giving rise to a myth.

Max Mueller called myth a "disease of language" (Mythology, Wikipedia 8). He was of the view that myths arose due to the lack of any form of language. The anthropologist James Frazer interpreted myths as "a misinterpretation of magical rituals". The twentieth century theories of myth have the most acceptable and practical approach of interpreting myths. The psychoanalysts like Sigmund Freud, Carl Jung and Claude Levi Strauss believed that "myths and dreams reveal unconscious psychological forces within people" (Mythology, Wikipedia, 7). Mark Schorer remarks in *William Blake: The Politics of Vision*:

Myth is fundamental, the dramatic representation of our deepest instinctual life..., capable of many configurations, upon which all particular opinions and attitudes depend (Guerin, 160)

Guerin aptly remarks that myths take their shapes from the cultural environments in which they grow. "Myth is ubiquitous in time as well as place. It is a dynamic factor everywhere in human society; it transcends time, uniting the past (traditional modes of belief) with the present (current values) and reaching toward the future (spiritual and cultural aspirations) (Guerin, 160).

The mythopoeic perspective has been most impressively represented in Northrop Frye's *Anatomy* of C*riticism*, which stands as the poetics of the entire mythopoeic movement. Frye asserts "In literary criticism myth ultimately means mythos, a structural organizing principle of literary form. He also endorses a view and argues that the monomyth is "the story of loss and regaining of identity".

This loss and regaining of identity is well exemplified by Karnad in *Hayavadana* through the incompleteness of *Hayavadana* who holds the central key of the play. Karnad in his plays presents an amalgam of facts and fantasy by combining and exploring the dramatic potential of the ancient Indian myths, legends and folk traditions. In a way Karnad has shown to the world theater community, how our past and present can coalesce to give a direction to theatre activities and how this fusion can add significance and meaning to our present day existence.

Karnad's drama bears out that cultural specificities cannot be ignored while formulating a theory of modernity. In this context, Charles Taylor's observations are highly pertinent. While arguing for what he terms a cultural theory of modernity, he says:

[T]ransitions to what we might recognize as modernity, taking place in different civilizations, will produce different results that reflect their divergent starting points. Different cultures' understandings of the person, social relations, states of mind, foods and bads, virtues and vices, and the sacred and profane are likely to be distinct. The future of our world will be one in which all societies will undergone change, in institutions and outlook, and some of these changes may be parallel, but they will not converge, because new differences will emerge from the old. (Mee, 17-18)

Similarly, in his essay Dilip Gaonkar advocates "a culture-specific reading of modernity" (18). The theatre of roots, therefore, says Erin B. Mee, "asserts an alternative notion of modernity and modern Indian theatre – one based on aesthetics derived from Indigenous Indian performance" (18). This assertion certainly does repudiate theatrical modernity but is a 'redfinition of it' (18).

Tylor also points out that alternative modernity "has to be able to relate both the pull of sameness and the forces making for difference" (18). He further says: "simply taking over Western Modernity couldn't be the answer... They have to invent their own."

In much the same manner, Dilip Gaonkar talks about creative adaptation, which according to him points to the manifold ways in which people question the present. It is the site where people make themselves modern, as opposed to being made modern by alien and impersonal forces and where they give themselves an identity and a destiny.

The roots movement like many other voices from the margin, questions the colonial cultural constructs of modernity as being the only notion of modernity. Providing alternatives, it goes a long way in establishing new definitions of modern Indian theatre. While defining the roots movement, caution has to be served vis-à-vis its nationalist stance. It must be remembered that it is not a revivalist movements. It is in essence, anti-colonial, but does not scorn the western dramaturgy. It simply creates one of its own. While doing so, it celebrates the regional developments in the Indian Theatre.

The relevance of the theatre of roots cannot be questioned. The drama of Karnad, Pannikar and Rattan Thiam bears out that while using traditional performances, their drama incorporates ideas and themes, very relevant to contemporary social set-up. The roots movement does not revive the past but gives it a contemporary meaning.

The present book takes into account the efforts of the exponents of the theatre of roots towards a redefinition of the Indian theatre in the modern times. The 'Introduction' traces the history of theatre in India by focusing at the outset on the *Natyashastra.* The theories of this fourteenth century compendium on theatre are particularly relevant in the context of the theatre of roots movement. Among other things the *Natyashastra* underscores the importance of the sutradhar, the dramatization of the myths and legends from the great Indian epics and the folk tales. This is particularly significant because the exponents of the theatre of roots movement also draw heavily on these aspects of the Indian theatre. The chapter also attempts to give an overview of the modern Indian theatre and its evolution in the twentieth century. The major features of the theatre of roots and its emphasis on performance are highlighted. Emphasis is also placed on the evolution of the movement and the efforts made by its major exponents to crystallize the theories underlining it.

The second chapter "Reconceptualizing Myths And Legends" defines myth at the outset. A classical as well as modern interpretation of myths is incorporated thereafter. The chapter examines three plays of Girish Karnad, *Yayati*,

The Fire And The Rain and Bali: The Sacrifice. The mythological tales are used in these plays as themes, subjects and source material. However, these epic tales are presented using the performance based oriental dramaturgy and the western techniques. The chapter underscores the fact that western dramaturgy alone inadequate for projecting social aspirations, cultural patterns and fundamental problems of contemporary India. The ritualistic and ceremonial aura of Karnad's play is discussed in the backdrop of the traditional Indian aesthetics with emphasis falling on the sense of performance rather than the text. The chapter also highlights the way myths not only make Karnad's plays more complex and richer but also the way myths are employed by him to foreground concerns that are intrinsically modern in spirit.

The third chapter 'Representing Modernity through Folk and Theatre' refers to the affinity of the roots movement with the traditional 'folk' forms of Indian theatre as well as the tradition of story-telling. The chapter otlines the conventions of folk theatre such as masks, mime, songs, the commentator-narrator or the *sutradhar* and the story within the story. Examing three plays of Karnad, *Hayavadana, Naga-Mandala and Flowers*, the chapter attempts to establish a connection between folk theatre/folk tales and complexities of modern existence as underlying themes of these plays. This chapter also like the previous one emphasizes the fact that the Indian folk theatre is a cultural metaphor that goes a long way in decolonizing the modern Indian theatre.

The fourth chapter 'Resurrecting History as Contemporaneity' aims to emphasize the fact that India is "an arena of cultural encounters", (Khilnani XIV), which are celebrated as creative and regenerative by the roots playwright. Karnad's fascination for the historical figures of the Mughal as well the pre-Mughal periods is taken into account. The chapter analyzes three plays of Karnad namely *Tughlaq, Tale-Danda* and *The Dreams of Tipu Sultan.* It is highlighted that the historical plays of Karnad not only strive to define the way the concept of nation came into being, but also underscore the importance of the historical past of cultural mixing. The chapter also focuses on the way the historical themes contribute towards creating a larger, Indian theatrical ethos, once again, decolonizing the theatre. One of the major ideas dealt with is that Karnad uses history as contemporaneity that is history's relevance to contemporary situations in foreground.

The conclusion sums up the major issues discussed in the earlier chapters. There is also an attempt to situate Karnad as a major exponent of the theatre of roots. The chapter also sums up the contribution of roots movement to the contemporary drama in India.

Chapter-2

Reconceptualising Myths and Legends

The theatre of roots movement was conceptualized by the modern Indian playwrights in order to strengthen India's cultural identity, by challenging the colonial aesthetics, thereby redefining the modern Indian theatre. After Independence, a number of playwrights turned to mythology, religious rituals and other Indian genres to create an indigenous Indian theatre. The roots playwrights felt that "... theatre forms borrowed from the west [were] totally inadequate for effectively projecting the social aspirations, way of life, cultural patterns and fundamental problems of contemporary India (Mee, 7)", and reverted to the ancient Hindu mythology and legends to re-present the past making it relevant to contemporary India.

Myths and legends are found all over the world; their origin and purpose form a special part of the story about the development of the human race. Some of these myths embody people's early explanations of the world they lived in. The forces which governed their lives were personified, given names and personalities. This was the first step to the formalization of belief in ritual and in religion leading to the emergence of galaxy of gods, devils, heroes and monsters out of various communities from different parts of the world. The word mythology has been derived from the Greek word *mythologia* which refers to a body of folklore, myths and legends that a particular culture believes to be true. The word myth in Greek meant "fable", "tale", "talk", or simply "speech", but it came to be used in contrast with logos and historian, thus coming to denote "that which cannot really exist." (Elaide, 37)

A myth within its extent provides justification for a religious belief, a ritual or a natural phenomenon. Myths are often narrated in legends, allegories and fables. Myths explain the origin of certain phenomena and tell us about the creation of the world of man and of animals. They explain why or how a certain natural event takes place. Myths also question the birth of rituals. They have a religious background, that is their principal actors must be gods or demigods. Each Indian myth celebrates the belief that the universe is boundless and things exist simultaneously depending upon each other. The epics and legends dating back over 3500 years continue to be told over and over again in temples, cities and villages of India. The old patterns and beliefs have been retained in folk tales and folk lore, which form the most vital and longest surviving system of mythology today.

Closely connected with myth is the word saga, Scandinavian in origin, which means a 'tale', or a 'story'. Both myth and saga form essential part of mythology. A myth explains a natural phenomenon, ritual or custom. The saga on the other hand, is more elaborate with a combination of folk-tale motifs and mythical ideas having some basis in fact.

The *Mahabharata*, the great epic of India, a compendium of over 100,000 verses interwoven with the main thread of the epic battle between the Pandavas and their cousins the Kauravas is a storehouse of legends. It comprises numerous myths as well as dynastic histories of obscure kings, explicit recipes for ritual offerings, hair splitting philosophical arguments, and tedious discussions of caste laws. The *Ramayana*, the other great Sanskrit epic, is far more consistent than the *Mahabharata*. It is shorter and more refined in its literary style. The most comprehensive sources of Hindu mythology are the eighteen great Puranas and the numerous minor Puranas which form the veritable encyclopaedia of Indian thought. The Puranas remain the basis of most 'modern' Hindu retellings of the myths, which deviate from the traditional texts.

A myth by its very nature does not have one single meaning. It is like a prism through which various shades of life are illuminated. Wendy O' Flaherty makes a level classification in her book *Hindu myths*. The first level is the narration wherein lies the story. Second is the divine level;

... which concerns mythology as it used to be understood by scholars of the classics, the metaphorical struggles of divine powers and personalities (Flaherty, 22).

The third is the cosmic level of the myth which is "the expression of universal laws and processes of metaphysical principles and symbolic truths" (Flaherty,22) Then comes the human level where myth merges into folklore, which involves the search for meaning in human life. Girish

Karnad's drama and the theatre of roots in general embody such merging of myth and folklore.

Myths have inherent ambiguity in them and are elusive. They have the fluidity of living organisms that change constantly. We can place myths "in the tantalizing realm of the occult"(Eliade,72) and think of myths as inspired fantasy. Myths provided earliest answers to the mysteries of the unknown. They are the very foundation of our culture and spiritual heritage. Therefore, myths blossomed into stories about divine or heroic beings. Some myths sprang from the oral tradition of storytelling and were later textualized. The origin myths or the creation myths, which describe the beginning of a custom or a tradition in a specific civilization, were derived from the sacred sources such as the *Ramayana*, the *Mahabharta*, the *Upanishads*, the *Vedas* and the *Puranas*.

Frazer's *The Golden Bough* (1890) broadened the scope and knowledge of myth and ritual. It further established the affinity between ritual, myth, dream and literature. Frazer in his book also asserted the importance of myth to a larger understanding of human culture. He agreed that myths are generated by many cultural needs. He remarks, "Myths authorize the cultural institutions of a tribe, a city, or a nation by connecting them with universal truths" (Quoted by Grebstein, 311).

The pre-modern theories interpret myths on account of historical events and various distortions occurred because of the telling and re-telling of myths. During the second half of the nineteenth century, an attempt was made to interpret myth scientifically. E.B. Taylor interpreted myth as an attempt at a literal explanation for natural phenomena. He speculated that early man attributed souls to inanimate objects and tried to explain natural phenomena thereby giving rise to a myth. At a psychological level C.G. Jung, projected an altogether different approach based on the theory of the collective unconscious. For him the mythical forms and images are present in every human being, resting in a state of potentiality and may become activated in myth or dream at any given moment. Thus, he explains myths as the expressions of "a primordial psychic process that may even precede the advent of the human race" (Eliade, 37).

Therefore, myths can be seen as a concept which can be related to the psychic processes governing mankind or as an explanation of some natural phenomena, mythic or historical, re-presented in stories about divine or heroic beings passed down traditionally. Age-old myths are told and retold with a vividness that retains their full power.

Myths constitute the very fabric of Indian life. Girish Karnad is among those distinguished playwrights who have mastered the art of transforming Indian folklore, mythological tales and historical episodes into thought provoking plays. Karnad has a remarkably powerful perception of the contemporary world and his works bring forth timeless truths in the shape of myths and folklore. He draws on the Indian mythology for his themes and puts these myths on trial. At times in Karnad's works history is subordinated to myth and at other times he transforms history into myth.

Being a part of the roots movement, Karnad celebrates the rich cultural heritage of the Indian classical Sanskrit drama and the folk tradition by incorporating rituals and traditions. The myths weave an intricate pattern in the play, making it more complex and richer. Karnad, however, does not employ mythological framework for its own sake. He uses myths to highlight certain concerns which are intrinsically modern in spirit.

Among the plays that have a powerful mythopoeic context are *Yayati, The Fire and the Rain, Bali: The Sacrifice* among others. The myth of Yayati has been dramatized by Karnad in his play *Yayati,* which glorifies the existentialist philosophy of the performance of duty and acceptance of responsibilities. *The Fire and the Rain* employs several myths and legends, each having a standpoint of its own, which refer to the central story. Karnad's disillusionment with dead and worn-our traditions is clearly discernible in the play. The play *Bali: The Sacrifice* is based upon the thirteenth-century Kannada epic, *Yashodhara* Charite. The myth of Cock of Dough has been used by Karnad to question the conflict and dilemmas inherent in the notion of non-violence propagated by Mahatma Gandhi. Karnad dwells upon the issue of violence and bloodshed involved in sacrifices. The play also condemns the intended violence as it carries within itself the original violent impulse.

Yayati : Metaphors of Immortality, Existentialism and Assertion

Yayati is Karnad's first play. The play has been translated into different Indian languages. Its revised English translation appeared in the year 2008. Yayati was the first play written by Karnad when he was twenty one years old and was about to leave for England on the Rhodes scholarship in 1962.

While I was writing the play, I saw it only as an escape from my stressful situation... the myth of Yayati reflected my anxieties at that moment, my resentment with all those who seemed to demand that I sacrifice my future. By the time I had finished working on Yayati… – the myth had enabled me to articulate to myself a set of values that I had been unable to arrive at rationally. Whether to return home finally seemed the most minor of issues; the myth had nailed me to my past (Chatterji, The Hindu Online,2).

In one of his essays Karnad again points out, "Going abroad was a much rarer experience in those days. Besides, I was the first member of a large close-knit family ever to go abroad. I wrote *Yayati* while preparing for the trip. The myth helped me to articulate my resentment at all those who seemed to demand sacrifice of my future." (Karnad, Yayati, 74).The play underscores the father son relationship and its mythic dimensions. However, Karnad does not lose sight of the relevance of the theme to modern times . The play therefore, has a universal appeal. As Jayant Kulkarni, who played *Yayati* in Karnataka Sangh production of the play points out, "Karnad has deftly explored various strands of the father-son relationship. Despite the mythological dramatic structure, I can easily relate to the Yayati-Puru entanglement. The playwright, who is questioning his past, has explored his insecurities through a classical plot" ( ).

Yayati is based on a tale found in the Mahabharata. The epic contains complex, intriguing and often enigmatic characters, who are fascinating and real. The story of Yayati as found in the original begins with his wife, Devayani, the beautiful daughter of Sukracharya, the preceptor of the Asuras (demons). Before her marriage, Devayani was insulted, slapped, and thrown into a (waterless) well by Sharmishtha, the daughter of the king of Asuras. Yayati, who happened to pass by, had rescued Devayani by holding her right hand and pulling her out of the well. Devayani had then asked Yayati to marry him. However, the prevailing custom of the day forbade a Kshatriya to marry a Brahmin girl (this was called the Pratiloma marriage); Yayati refused, stating the Pratiloma rule as the obstacle for their marriage.

Seething with rage, Devayani complained to her father about Sharmishtha. Sukracharya, who loved his only daughter dearly told the king that he would leave the kingdom if his daughter was not appeased. Devayani also set her condition for revenge. Sharmishtha had to be her 'dasi' and serve her in the house she would occupy after her marriage. Sharmishtha yielded in order to save her father's honour. Yayati later married Devayani after Sukracharya agreed to make an exception to the Pratiloma rule. The rule was bent for the sake of his daughter's happiness.

In course of time, Sharmishtha was attracted to Yayati and asked him to marry her. A bewitching beauty, Yayati found her hard to resist. He made her his queen and gave Devyani the status of senior queen. Devayani complained bitterly to her father and a furious Sukracharya cursed him with old age. This is the crucial juncture of Yayati's story. An extremely sensual king, Yayati believed in enjoying all the pleasures that life could offer a king. And this curse left him distraught. Sukracharya, the sage later mellowed and told him that if anybody was willing to exchange his youth for Yayati's old age, Yayati's youth would be restored. Yayati approached each of his sons and asked them about this bargain. None except Pooru agreed. When a delighted Yayati embraced Pooru, the transfer was complete. Pooru became a ripe old man in the prime of his youth, while Yayati regained his youth.

Yayati pursued pleasure with a renewed zest. The original *Mahabharata* tells us that the more he indulged, the thirstier he grew. Finally tired of his own youth, he asked Pooru to take back his youth. In the original *Mahabharta*, King Yayati tells Pooru that sensual desire is never quenched by indulgence. He argues that no object of desire—corn, gold, cattle, women – nothing can ever satisfy the desire. This according to him, is the state of Brahmanism of man. One can find peace only by a mental poise that goes beyond likes and dislikes. Saying thus, Yayati had asked Pooru to take back his youth. Yayati then retired to the forest to perform penance. In due course, he attained the perfect state of Brahmanism.

Karnad's Yayati is similarly stricken with an overwhelming desire for indulgence. Since Karnad potrays him as an existential king, he alters Yayati's character. He casts Pooru also in a similar mould. Pooru is the eternal conflict-torn drama protagonist, who in this play, vacillates between the desire to reclaim his youth and fulfilling his duty as a son. In Karnad's *Yayati*, the story seems to lean heavily in favour of Pooru not Yayati. In the original, Pooru's role begins with accepting his father's old age with respectful dignity and ends with returning it. Pooru never thinks twice, he doesn't crib, and most importantly, is not in a dilemma, whether he made the right choice or not.

But Karnad's Pooru is after all more human, tender hearted and feels dejected about the loss of his youth. His mental anguish desperately needs an outlet. He expresses his anxiety in a few monologues and asides. However, this poses a problem because in the original, there is a limited emphasis on Pooru's role and character. The playwright, therefore, needs to strengthen, enhance, and add more significance to Pooru so that his presence can be felt. In other words, Karnad's Pooru needs to be treated with greater importance as well as compassion. Karnad once remarked in an interview:

I was also intrigued by the idea that if Pooru had a wife, How would she react? I introduced Chitralekha. Every character in the play tries to evade the consequences of their action, except Sharmishtha and Chitralekha (Mukherji, 31).

In the play, Chitralekha is presented as Pooru's wife – a character who is absent in the original story of Yayati. Chitralekha commits suicide in the play when she learns that Pooru has traded his youth for old age. Karnad also underplays Yayati's confession that indulgence does not lead to peace and happiness. Thus, Karnad's hero is Pooru, not Yayati. Karnad's Yayati comes across as merely a pleasure-monger while in the original, his character is symbolic of a higher ideal of one striving for truth, and eternal happiness, a mighty invincible hero, descendent of the Kuru dynasty. Yayati's long span of sensual indulgence is a symbol that indicates the futility of chasing happiness in things that come to an end. Indulgence only increases thirst, it does not satisfy it. Each moment of happiness ends with the lament that it is over, leading to a desire to experience the pleasure once more. Yayati's disillusionment is complete only with saturation. He has had his fill but remains unfulfilled. Which is what plods him to seek a non-cyclical happiness. Harbans Singh in his article "Quest for the Carnal" rightly calls it the "…Yayati syndrome, the unending search for carnal satiation that explores the underbelly of human beings" (Singh, Quest, 4).

Thus, Karnad's Yayati retells the age old story of the mythological King who in his longing for eternal youth sought to borrow the vitality of his own son. In the original version, neither Yayati nor his son suffer from any kind perplexity or dilemma. They are aware of their motivations, their choices, and have great conviction. They feel no guilt or remorse. Pooru considers it his filial duty towards his father, adhering firmly to the dictum of *pitru devo bhava* (father is god). Yayati's character is highlighted when he expresses his desire to eternally indulge in sensual pleasures. However, his strength of character is exhibited when he speaks with conviction that he has had enough of that. It should be remembered that Yayati, before asking Pooru had approached his other three sons who all refused to comply with his request. The expectation part falls flat. Yayati's was a request, not a command, which is why his other three sons were completely free to refuse. Pooru, like his elder brothers was completely free to refuse Yayati's request. He freely chose to take on his father's old age.

Influenced by the existentialist drama, *Yayati* explores the complexities of responsibility and expectations within the Indian family. Drawing on a myth from the *Mahabharata*, Karnad expresses in it a personal dilemma between his family's demands and his own wish for freedom. When asked about the presence of existentialist strains in the play, Karnad had commented:

It is true that existentialism was the persuasive philosophy of the time. My attempt was to emphasise the calm acceptance of grief and anguish. Pooru's old age is a sudden transformation and not the eventuality of life. It brings no wisdom and no self-realisation. It is a senseless punishment for an act he has not committed. (Mukherji, 31)

As pointed out earlier, when Karnad was at Dharwad and preparing to leave for England he was in a dilemma about his future. Karnad agrees that *Yayati* echoes existentialists views like that of Sartre and Camus. In one of his interviews, Karnad says:

I was excited by the story of Yayati, this exchange of ages between the father and the son, which seemed to me terribly powerful and terribly modern. At the same time I was reading a lot of Sartre and the existentialists. This consistent harping on responsibility which the existentialists indulge in suddenly seemed to link up with the story of Yayati. (Suneel, 126)

Yayati is hailed as the first modern play in the history of Kannada theatre. The audience in the West on whom Karnad aimed to create an impact was largely ignorant of the vast and awe-inspiring Indian mythology and its various subtleties. For a man like Karnad, well-versed in English literature and western philosophy, rendering Yayati in an existential form proved fruitful.

The most recent English translation of the play by Karnad was published in the year 2008. Earlier the play was translated into English by Priya Adarkar and published in *Enact* in 1961. For some reasons he felt uncomfortable with the work and decided to treat it as part of his juvenilia. The urge to meddle with it was irresistible for Karnad though he thought it would be disastrous to tackle a play written at the age of twenty- two at the age of sixty-nine. The Prologue to the play captures attention and is of great importance . The Sutradhar addresses the audience and begins by explaining the meaning and significance of the word 'sutradhar':

Good evening, I am the Sutradhar, which literally means 'the holder of strings'....the string being the instrument of measurement, actually points to my descent from the carpenter, the prop-maker or the architect. In effect, I am the person who has conceived the structures here, whether of brick and mortar or of words. I have designed and consecrated the stage. I am responsible for the choice of the text. And here I am now, to introduce the performance and to insure that it takes place without any hindrance. (Karnad, *Yayati*, 5)

The elucidation here not only brings out the importance and relevance of the narrator, the Sutradhar, in this play but has a wider implication as the Sutradhar is an integral feature of most of Karnad's plays. We are then told by the Sutradhar that the play deals with an ancient myth but it is not "mythological". According to the Sutradhar a mythological play aims to make us believe that the sole reason for our sufferings in this world is that we have forsaken our gods and all sufferings is:

... devised by the gods, to check out our willingness to submit to their will. If we crush our egos and give ourselves up in surrender, divine grace will descend upon us and redeem us. (6)

The Sutradhar further adds that "there are no deaths in mythologicals ...death cannot give meaning to anything that has gone before. It merely empties life of meaning"(6).The metaphor of death here is suggestive of the ongoing events in the play. Karnad further strengthens the metaphor in one of the most important speeches by King Yayati in the play, Yayati moralises and says:

I thought there were two options – life and death. No, it is living and dying we have to choose between... dying can go on for all eternity. (68)

The Sutradhar then tells the audience that the play has no gods and it deals with death. The key element in the plot being the " '*Sanjeevani*' *vidya*-- the art of reviving the dead, which promises release from the limitations of the fleeting life this soul is trapped in"(6). To posses this art the gods and the 'rakshasas' have been killing each other and the humans have been trying to master it. We aspire to become immortals but cannot achieve the power necessary to understand eternity. "Death eludes definition. Time coils into a loop, reversing the order of youth and old age. Our certainties crumble in front of the dark demands of the heart" (6).

Karnad has very aptly summed up the entire idea behind writing the play and also refers to the use of myth of Yayati. No one else but King Yayati is the apt mythological figure, who could well illustrate the point, Karnad wanted to make. He returns to the "...ancient lore not because it offers any blinding revelation or hope of consolation, but because it provides fleeting glimpses of the fears and desires sleepless within us. It is a good way to get introduced to ourselves" (6).

The theme and purpose of the play are, thus, revealed through the character of the Sutradhar who tries to bridge the gap between the audience and the stage. He adds that it is a mythical play – a page from the history of the unknown:

When you follow the trail of the past you're like a lost wayfarer, groping in a huge cavern filled with the ruins of an old and unfamiliar mode of life .You grope...and you must listen to the call of the past, give it the ears of the present. The result is the story of our ancestors, but we see our own image there. (6)

The hidden contemporary undertones are brought to the surface as we read and experience the story of Yayati as re-told by Karnad. He has given a new meaning to the past and has tried to re-interpret the ancient lore in a modern perspective. Karnad ends the Prologue by saying that "We must re-live, not a saga embedded in books, but a tale orally handed down by our grandmothers in lamp lit corners." He adds that we must trust the narrative and "Invent bits if necessary, but go on" (6).

We are thereby prepared to be transported to the past and taken into the inner chamber of King Yayati's palace. Prince Pooru, the King's son is returning home after many years of absence, with his bride Chiralekha, the Princess of Anga. Crowd around the palace is eagerly waiting to see the royal couple. The Sutradhar comments in the prologue:

The two must enter this space and on this bed they must create for themselves the magic kingdom of love, ambition and power. He must sow his seed here and then launch forth on a campaign of victory and death. She must proudly bear on her breasts the tooth marks incised by their offspring. Must. Nothing, however, ever happens as it must.(6)

The future is being predicted that nothing ever happens as we wish it to be . We are also informed that what we have in front of us is "...not a well-charted map but a network of paths, many of which plunge into the shrubbery and disappear before we have even registered them"(6).

The four skilfully crafted acts of the play sum up the story of King Yayati and Pooru. Many issues are brought forth by

Karnard. One among them is the caste conflicts between the Kshatriyas, the Brahmins and the Rakshasas. While Indian mythology forms the backbone of the play, Karnad's modifications lend a special touch to the known story. The action begins on an important day in King Yayati's life. His son Pooru is expected to arrive at the palace. Queen Devyani has asked two maids Swarnalata and Sharmishtha to deck up his chamber. A quarrel ensues between the duo and leads to the unravelling of the old rivalry between Devyani and Sharmishtha. The play starts with Devyani and Swarnlata in King's chamber where Swaranlata is upset and talking about 'the Rakshasi', that is Sharmishtha, who doesn't accord proper respect to Devyani. She complains about Sharmishtha's nasty jibes and calls her " spiteful whore" and tells Devyani that she is afraid of her; she further adds: "It is not Sharmishtha's nastiness that one has to be wary of. It is her uncanny ability to cut close to the bone…" (8).

It is revealed that Sharmishtha and Devyani were once very good friends. Devyani, therefore, stops Swaranlata by saying that she has known her for years and they should not waste time talking about her. Devyani tells her: 'Remember, it is an important day in my life' as Pooru is returning home with his wife, and asks her to leave and ready their chamber. Devyani feels depressed by Swaranlata's talk and asks Shamishtha as to why she troubles Swaranlata. Sharmishtha replies that she was not being deliberately nasty: "It is just that I am an uncouth rakshasi. And the situation here…a Kshatriya palace, ruled over by a Brahmin queen! Confusing isn't the world" (9).

Sharmishtha argues with Devyani and asks her to remember the old times and says:

You were the offspring of a destitute Brahmin, dependent upon my father. I had everything. Beauty, education, wealth. Everything except birth--an Arya pedigree. What was your worth? That your father knew the 'sanjeevani' spell. That is all (10).

According to Sharmishtha, Yayati , whom he calls the 'scion of the Bharata dynasty' is not short of women but he chose Devyani to be his wife because only she could 'lead him to the ultimate goal', that is, to become immortal. One of the key themes in the play is the powerful human desire to attain immortality. The Sutradhar refers to it, at the outset:

Our play has no go gods. And it deals with death. A key element in its plot is the 'Sanjeevani' Vidya – the art of reviving the dead, which promises release from the limitations of the fleeting life this self is trapped in... Humans have been struggling to master it. Sadly, we aspire to become immortal but cannot achieve the lucidity necessary to understand eternity. Death eludes definition. Time coils into a loop, reversing the order of youth and old age. Our certainties crumble in front of the stark demands of the heart. (6)

Sharmishtha cannot forget that it was Yayati's desire to attain immortality which made him choose Devyani as his wife. She elaborates:

Sharmishtha: Yayati. The Scion of the Bharata dynasty. He is not short of women, is he? Women of his own kind. Sensuous Kshatriya maidens. Virgins reared for him. But he chooses you. Why? You know the answer. You, only you, could lead him to the ultimate goal: a sanctuary beyond the reach of death. Ah! The joy of turning the funeral pyres of one's kinsmen into altars for one's own fire sacrifice. The timeless thrill of it. (11)

Sharmishtha is full of spite for Devayani and makes highly provocative statements – all aimed at proving that it was Yayati's desire for immortality that led him to accept Devyani's love. When Devyani insists that the King loves her and that she is lusted for by him. Sharmishtha snaps, "Except that he is not lusting for you, you poor darling, he lusts for immortality. Your father's art of 'sanjeevani' (11). Sharmishtha further lends credence to this idea:

I have seen my father drugged on that ambition, panting for that supreme privilege. And now I see him in Yayati, who has the world in his palm. And your father, the great Shukracharya, has the means to keep it there. For eternity. That is what he lusts for (12).

Devyani chides Sharmishtha reminding her of the futility of her efforts, "Can't you see that you are only hurting yourself? Can't you see the futility of it all? Why don't you just open your eyes and see? To this Sharmistha replies:

I opened my eyes, two years ago. Don't you remember? I do. The precise moment. When I closed my eyes, I was the princess of the rakshasa... I opened my eyes. You had become the Queen of the Arya race. (10)

The play focuses on the question of race as no other play of Karnad does. Fanon observes that "however lacking in objective reality racist ideas... were, the psychological force of their construction of self meant that they acquired an objective existence in and through the behaviour of people" (Ashcroft, 205). Consequently the construction of the self, so made becomes a determinant reflected in the social and psychological behaviour of people. Sharmistha's comments about herself, about Yayati and about Devyani reflect this idea of self-image that in turn is reflected in her defiance and subservience in turn:

You Aryas have sorted out things so neatly for yourselves that we must seem confused. And confusing. Why does she behave like that? Why can't she see what is good for her? The answer, sir, is because we rakshasas have chosen to live in chaos, proud that it is a chaos of our own creation. And yet of course we also despise ourselves for not being lucid and rational, like you Aryas.

(Pause)

To be thus convoluted is our prerogative. (18)

Karnad had invested the play with complex issues concerning the fallout of interaction between the dominant and subjugated cultures. Sharmistha refers to her state of being in complete abandon before she met Devyani. She exclaims that she "was a perfect rakshasa princess-- spoilt, proud," who liked being with other rakshasa girls and boys, go singing and dancing with them, but "outside that world, conscious every moment, that we were rakshasas, held in contempt" (19). Then came Devyani into her life: "She was unlike any woman I had met. She seemed completely unconscious of the fact that she belonged to a superior race" (19).

Sharmistha thereafter narrates another incident, when both of them were lying in the sun not knowing their blouses had been exchanged. Devyani realized this and woke her up. Sharmishtha was somewhat annoyed as she was on the brink of a beautiful dream. Devyani, according to Sharmishtha, reacted unexpectedly:

Sharmishtha: You poor people; she said. And I realized with rising panic that she had never ever used that phrase before. Never talked of us in plural. 'You poor people. You only have to get into a piece of Arya attire. And you start fantasizing' (20).

Sharmishtha's words have the desired effect on Yayati: "I came to reprimand you. But now I am lost for words."

Karnad's plays have a mythological framework but they are intrinsically modern in spirit vis-à-vis their treatment of issues of contemporary value. *Yayati* not only deals with racism as it has existed since the earliest times but also highlights the fact that race "and racial prejudice in their modern forms have been intimately bound up with the colonial form of the institution of slavery, to the degree that it seems impossible to disentangle them" (Ashcroft, 214).

On being accused by Yayati that she "behaves like a cheap harridan! Sharmishtha brings to the fore a significant aspect of a slave's life:

You own hundreds of slaves. But have you ever wondered what it does to a person to be made a slave? It turns that person into an animal. A domesticated animal. One's will to act is destroyed. One's selfhood humbled into grateful submission. 'Accept that crumb, wait for a pat on the back.' To be a good slave is to have all your vileness extracted from you. (17)

Sharmishtha after narrating the whole incident, with a light heart tells Yayati that all these years she needed someone to listen to her and is grateful to Yayati that he has. She also tells Yayati that her father had given her a vial of poison so that she can consume it if she were to return home. She tries to kill herself by consuming it when Yayati stops her and holds her right hand. She says: "you are holding my right hand and I am a princess". She adds that she doesn't want to trap him in her words. It is under these circumstances that Yayati's heart melts for Sharmishtha, which results in establishing an intimate relation between the two. Sharmishtha initially seems to be reluctant and says that "I am not going to share a bed" as sharing the palace with Devyani has been very unpleasant. Devyani happens to listen to all this conversation and orders Sharmishtha to leave the palace and also frees her from being her slave. Sharmishtha conceitedly tells Devyani "Yes, I got him into bed with me. That was my revenge on you. After all , as a slave, what weapon did I have but my body". Yayati intervenes and tells Devyani that he is going to marry Sharmishtha and will make her his queen. He also assures Devyani by saying:

... Your position will not be touched. You will remain the Senior Queen. You will share my throne. You will be at my side in all public celebrations… She can never be a threat to your position, you know that, because of her race. (29)

For Yayati, Devyani remains important because she is the daughter of Shukracharya and he cannot think of incurring his wrath and therefore keeps her as his senior Queen. Sharmishtha being a rakshasa princess cannot become the queen of the Aryas so he found a way out. However, race can never be erased from one's identity. Sharmishtha has cast a spell on Yayati. He is bewitched by her beauty but he must never forget that she belongs to an inferior race. The play once again foregrounds the issue of race and gender exploitation. Yayati has no qualms over possessing both women who are pitted against each other, primarily because both covet him.

The subject of caste and race is vitally important to the play. We are told that Pooru is the son of a Rakshasa princess and considers himself "A half-caste. A mongrel". Swaranlata reveals that Pooru is not the real son of Devyani and that she had pledged to be his mother when she had become the queen. He wants to break the deathly silence that surrounded his mother as no one in the palace ever talks about her. Yayati had met Pooru's mother in a military campaign. He had never seen anyone so beautiful—ethereal. He adds, "She gave me a son and I made her my Senior Queen". Suddenly she changed and started screaming as if she had gone mad and told Yayati that she wanted to make life miserable for everyone in the palace. It was in her last days on bed that she told Yayati that she was a rakshasa woman and the Aryas had once destroyed her home and in vengeance she had made sure that the Crown prince of the Bharatas had rakshasa blood in him. It is now that Pooru says that the prince of the Aryas has polluted blood in his veins and that he is a mongrel. He bursts into a derisive laughter and calls it "excruciatingly thrilling". He tells Yayati that he despises him and hates him for all this hypocrisy.

At this juncture, Pooru and Chitralekha enter the palace and the welcome rites are performed. Pooru then briefs Yayati about how his wedding took place. Chitralekha's father had organised an archery contest for princes all over the land which had to be cancelled at the eleventh hour, as they received reports about Pooru's skill and thus they decided that Chitralekha should marry the Bharata prince. Pooru remarks that they actually did not need me, they needed a male figure from this palace and even "a door keeper's statue would have done just as well". Yayati is annoyed at this and Pooru calms him by saying that it is a fact and Chitralekha herself has told him this. He proudly says:

That is what I like about her: she is intelligent, loving, and full of fun; but also honest and practical. She accepts me as I am, a fact to live with (37).

Pooru's dilemma has been handled by Girish Karnad in an existential vein. Pooru articulates his choices clearly, the primacy of which is most important to him than the system which dictates his life. He tells Yayati about his disillusionment with his ancestors, whose deeds he found pompous. For him, to be in his room and to brood over his mother's memory, means everything. Pooru would eventually like to go away leave everything but not before he provides Chitralekha with a son.

Pooru:I want to have a son as she will have no grumble against me. Nor will anyone else. I can place him in her arms, under your tender care and leave. He can take after his ancestors

Yayati:And you?

Pooru:How shall I put it? My forefathers were the great eagles, keen eyed, hovering regally in the clouds. I shall seek to be a worm. (27)

Yayati then tells him about Swaranlata's husband who was a charioteer who decided to be a worm but "went berserk—women, drinks, asceticism, opiates." Nothing brought him peace and he finally committed suicide .The irony of the situation is that no one told this to Swaranlata and she still dresses up like a married women. When Yayati asks Pooru as to where would he go if he were to become a worm. Pooru once again articulates his existential choice:

You think everyone has a readymade answer. I just want to go somewhere where I can sit quietly and ask myself questions. Just ask questions. Not seek answers. Ask questions of myself. I should be quite content if I found the right question. Just one. (38)

When Sharmishtha comes running and pleads before Pooru, saying that only he can save his majesty as Shukracharya has cursed Yayati that he will lose his youth and become decrepit by nightfall. Pooru is baffled and is not aware as to why Devyani has gone to Shukracharya. Yayati loses his mind and is astounded by the thought of it. "Old age! Decrepitude! By nightfall! And then?" He holds Sharmishtha responsible for all this and calls her a she – devil, who has trapped him with her wiles. She asks him to be patient but Yayati answers:

Patience? Patience of a man falling into a bottomless pit. Patience? The deafening rush of emptiness. What can be more terrible than that? (42)

Sharmishtha tries to pacify him and asks him to accept it and go away from the city and says that she is ready to share the wilderness with him; she tells him that "No one can escape old age. You have just hastened its arrival" (42). Yayati cannot bear think of the horror of it and says that that he has gathered the rarest moments of his life like precious stones so that he could play with them, relive them. Sharmishtha tells him that for him everything has been a game, an object 'to be used and discarded'. She asks him to go and seek for more important things in solitude. This infuriates Yayati:

Solitude? What are you talking about? I don't want solitude. I can't bear it. I want people around me. Queens, ministers, armies, enemies, the populace. I love them all. Solitude? The very thought is repulsive. If I have to know myself, Sharmishtha, I have to be young. I must have my youth. (43)

He tries to recapture his youth and remembers the moments when he "slaughtered enemies, razed hostile cities to ground, made my queens writhe in pain and demanded that they laugh and make love to me in gratitude" (43). Yayati even doubts that Pooru would be ready to take the curse on him he says that he must be happy with his youth and his chance to rule the world. He is suspicious because Pooru has Rakshasa blood in his veins and Yayati therefore does not trust him. This is where Yayati fails to understand Pooru's greatness and stoicism.

Yayati is shocked to know that no one among his subjects is ready to accept the King's burden. Pooru tells him that his people are of the view that the King has enjoyed the glory and that they have paid the taxes and tributes for the King's service. He fails to believe this and says: "No one? What do you mean by no one? My dear subjects for whose sake I have faced the thousand deaths?" (47). Yayati even thinks of bribing his people by saying that their families will be looked after . He even promises to give them all the fame and glory they want. But all this is of no use; utterly helpless and says:

Why ? Are the deeds of glory dead in this world? Has the world become so cynical, so corrupted that there is no place for… for… (47)

Karnad experiments audaciously with an age old myth making it relevant to the present –day scenario. Pooru then tells Yayati that his people have refused to talk to him as if he was offering them plague. No one wanted to discuss the big words like 'Trust? Glory? Sacrifice?'. Pooru suggests Yayati to do what Sharmishtha has recommended, that is to 'accept the inevitable'. For Yayati it was like stumbling down a road where there is no light, no hope. He bursts into tears and Pooru 'in a matter of fact voice' says:

Pooru : There is one person who is willing to take the curse

Yayati: There is ? Why didn't you say so? Who is it?

Pooru : A worm, aspiring to outdo the eagles. (49)

Yayati took a while to understand that Pooru is referring to himself and then asks him to shut up and refuses to talk to him. Sharmishtha is astouned by Pooru's decision and calls it 'utter stupidity' and adds that "...the desire for self–sacrifice is a rank perversion" (50). Pooru explains to Sharmishtha:

Pooru : I want to root myself back in my family. I want to realize the vision that drove my ancestors.

Sharmishtha : What about Chitralekha?

Pooru: I am like an infant on the brink of birth. Please don't shove me back with that name (50).

Pooru's choice is conscious and yet it is the fallout of the circumstances, he is surrounded with. When Yayati is cursed by Shukracharya the existential slant becomes even sharper. At the same time, however, the notion of responsibility is interrogated. On the one hand, Pooru makes a conscious choice to take the curse of decrepitude that Shukracharya placed on Yayati for humiliating Devyani and is apparently responsible for his decision. On the other, his actions have brought total disorder and defy logical explanation as he is totally unmindful of the consequences of his choice for Chitralekha.

Girish Karnad has invested Chitralekha's character with the note of self-assertion—an idea that is intrinsically modern. In the original version of the story in the *Mahabharata*,

Chitralekha does not exist. Karnad, however, created Chitralekha to emphasize the fact that Pooru's decision to exchange his youth for his father's old age could not have had implications for him alone. In order to embrace martyrdom, he brings immeasurable agony for Chitralekha. In spite of putting up a brave face, Chitralekha is deeply hurt. No one understands her pain except Swarnlata, who is herself a victim of cruel fate.

Swaranlata asks her not to hold back her tears, and says. "Cry, madam, please. Don't hold back your tears. Nothing is more harmful than suppressed tears"(55). Chitralekha tells her that she was wrong to considered Pooru an ordinary man and she is blessed to have him as her husband. Swaranlata leaves a couple of lights burning in then nuptial chamber as Chitralekha wishes to dazzle her 'eyes with his glory'. Pooru enters the chamber and "he is bent double, When he speaks, his voice is feeble and quivers with exhaustion"(56). He asks Chitralekha to forgive him as he didn't consult her before taking the decision. He tells Chitralekha:

This is no ordinary old age, devi. This is decrepitude. The sum total of Father's transgressions. The burden of the whole dynasty, perhaps. I couldn't take it on without your help. (57)

Chitralekha assures him that she has no life apart from him and says that she is privileged. She expresses her desire to perform the arati. The light causes irritation to Pooru's eyes and he asks her to hurry up. But as she moves the lamp in a circle in front of him, performing the arati she is terrified to see the 'withered features' of Pooru's face. She screams and drops the lamp on the floor. Screaming, she requests Pooru not to come near her, not to touch her. She asks him to forgive her and to go out. Chitralekha bursts into tears and Swaranlata tries to console her. Chitralekha blames her and says that she is not worthy of him and asks Swaranlata to kill her and punish her. Later, when she confronts a hypocritical Yayati. Chitralekha declares emphatically: "I will not let my husband step back into my bedroom unless he returns a young man" (61).

Swaranlata then narrates her own life story to Chitralekha telling her how she has been living with a lie that her husband is alive. She also tells her how she lied to her husband about her being seduced by one of her teachers. Swaranlata's husband could not accept this reality and disappeared forever. She waited for him but finally consoled herself with the hope that he had found peace in death. She makes a significant remark which once again refers to the metaphor of death in the play:

That is the great thing about death, isn't it? The assurance of peace, the deliverance from uncertainty (60).

Swaranlata adds that sometimes a distant cry from another unhappy soul helps. She narrates her story to divert Chitralekha's mind. Swaranlata then gives her the vial of poison which she has found while cleaning the room. This vial of poison belongs to Sharmishtha who was about to consume it when Yayati stopped her. He asks her to display self control as she is an educated woman. He asks her to welcome and escort Prince Pooru. When Chitralekha is reminded by Yayati walk in Pooru's footprints: "Whether home or into the wilderness," she says: "Or into funeral pyre" (62). At this Yayati exclaims that she "dare indulge in levity" about her husband's death, Chitralekha flares up, saying:

I did not push him to the edge of the pyre, sir. You did. You hold forth on my wifely duties. What about your duty to your son? Did you think twice before foisting your troubles on a pliant son? (62)

On being shouted at by Yayati, she once again has the courage to show him his place:

Sir! This is my chamber. Only my husband has the right to come in here without my permission. Or to shout out my name when he pleases. I am not aware I have allowed anyone else that freedom. (62)

She then shows Yayati the two gifts that greeted her as his daughter-in-law. Firstly, the pendant from the marriage thread of the Bharata queens which belongs to her mother-in-law (Devyani) who has discarded her and she found it lying on the floor in the room and secondly the vial of poison from the mother-in-law to be (Sharmishtha).

Yayati is lost for words and is 'genuinely anguished'. He tries to make her understand that it was Pooru's 'free will' and he never thought that he would accept the curse. Yayati tells her that he wanted to present a peaceful and prosperous kingdom to Pooru but he is engulfed in unexpected troubles. There are enemies on the border and rebellious forest tribes are also after him and there is the prospect of a famine which is causing him troubles and the danger of rakshasa depredation. According to Yayati Pooru lacks experience and cannot tackle these problems and therefore he needs Chitralekha's help. Yayati asks Chitrlekha to give time to Pooru , Chitrlekha then questions Yayati that has he thought how old she would be by the time a safe future would be secured? Yayati answers " Only a few years. Say a decade. Or even just four or five." Chitralekha laughs at this and says:

Four or five! Do you think it would make a difference if it were only one or two? This morning I was the mistress of all that I had yearned for. But within half a day--no, within half an hour actually - half a century has driven across my bed and crushed the dreams on my pillow. And you want me to wait... (65).

Yayati asks her to " rise above trivialities" and to be a superhuman. Chitrlekha agrees and says:

All right, your Majesty, I shall try. But when I do so, please don't try to dodge behind your own logic.

She calls him to accept the challenge as no one has ever faced a situation like this before. Chitralekha tells him that she married Pooru for his youth and now as he is old he does not possess the "potential to plant the seed of the Bharatas" in her womb. But Yayati has that potential. Yayati is shocked , Chitralekha explains her point that Yayati has taken over Pooru's youth and therefore he "should accept everything that comes attached to it". Yayati calls her a "whore", a "beast" and asks her if she is inviting him for fornication. Chitralekha now counterpoints him and says:

Oh, come, sir. These are trite considerations .We have to rise above such trivialities. We have to be superhuman. Nothing like this has ever happened before. Nothing like this is likely to… (66)

Chitralekha helplessly tells him that he can neither return her Pooru's youth and nor even accept her logic. She adds that, " It is part of the sacrifice which we all have to make" She picks up the vial of poison and holds it up to him and asks him "What else is there for me to do? You have your youth. Prince Pooru has his old age. Where do I fit in?"(66). Chitralekha swallows the poison, crumples with pain and collapses. She screams in Swaranlata's arms "Help me. Please. Don't let me die. I Don't want to die. Swaru, Swaru, help."(67) Swaranlata cries because she couldn't save her. Chitralekha could not get peace even in death. "There is no release in death,"(68) remarks Sharmishtha and sarcastically tells Yayati:

So here is the foundation of your glorious future, your Majesty. A woman dead, another gone mad, and a third in danger of her life. Goodbye, sir .(68)

Saying this Sharmishtha leaves. Yayati stands staring at Chitralekha and demented Swaranlata .In a long soliloquy Yayati speaks:

I thought there were two options- life and death. No, it is living and dying we have to choose between. And you have shown me that dying can go on for all eternity. Suddenly, I see myself, my animal body frozen in youth, decaying, deliquescing, turning rancid. You are lying on your pyre, child burning for life while I sink slowly in this quagmire, my body wrinkleless and grasping, but unable to grasp anything (68).

Sharmishtha leads Pooru in and Yayati asks Pooru to take back his youth, he says " Let me turn my decrepitude into a beginning. Pooru asks why? He then sees Chitralekha and Yayati tells him that she has killed herself. Sharmishtha calls her "The first martyr to His Majesty's glorious vision" . Yayati pleads before Pooru to take back his youth and to rule well. Yayati now wishes to face his destiny in the wilds. Yayati embraces Pooru and as they part Pooru becomes young again and Yayati is bent with old age. Yayati and Sharmishtha leave. Pooru touches their feet and then goes where Chitralekha is lying and says:

We brought you here only to die. But our senses are blighted and we shall never grasp the meaning of all that you taught us .(69)

Yayati has some remarkable women characters, who have mind of their own and refuse to be cowed down or silenced in the face of deprivation. Aparna Dharwadkar observes:

The most memorable feature of *Yayati* – and a striking accomplishment for a twenty two years old author – is its quarter of sentiment, articulate, embittered women, all of whom are subject in varying degrees to the whims of men, but succeed in subverting the male world through an assertion of their own rights and principles...(Karnad, Introduction Collected Plays, Vol. II, viii)

As the play comes to an end, Karnad's play once again borders on the tragic vision of the existentialists. Having regained his youth, Pooru is confounded as Chitralekha lies dead in front of him. He suddenly calls out to the heavens and questions "What does all this mean, O God? What does it mean? The Sutradhar enters and while he speaks Pooru lifts Chitralekha up and exits, followed by Swaranlata. The Sutradhar says that Pooru at last found the courage to ask a question:

But was it really a meaningful question or was it a cry of despair that he could hope for no meaning?...So let us assume that this question led to many more and that finally Pooru found the question he was seeking (70).

In compliance with the Sanskrit drama as a convention the play requires to have a happy ending. Therefore he asks us, the audience, to assume that this question led to many more. The Sutradhar adds that "…on the authority of the epics" it is believed that Pooru "ruled long and wisely and was hailed as a philosopher king" (70). With a Namaskar the Sutradhar exits.

Karnad has given new meaning and significance to the tale which is relevant to modern times. But by doing so he keeps intact the symbolic theme of Yayati's attachment to life and its pleasures. In the *Mahabharata*, Yayati recognizes the nature of desire itself and realises that fulfilment does not diminish or finish desire. In Karnad's play however, Yayati recognises the horror of his own life and assumes his moral responsibility after a series of symbolic encounters.

V.S. Khandekar, the eminent Marathi novelist, also used the Yayati myth in his novel *Yayati.* He focuses on the two important women in Yayati's life. As he explains in the introduction to the novel, he does not follow the story of Yayati as written in the Aadi Parva of Mahabharata. He creates his own version and interpretation of the characters and situations following the examples of Kalidas. Khandekar's Yayati represents a modern man who in spite of receiving much happiness in life remains restless and discontented. The mythical Yayati ran after sensual pleasures but Khandekar's Yayati runs after all kinds of materialistic pleasures. Though the tale is culled from the purans Khandekar's Yayati is a modern man (Singh, Quest, 4). In Karnad's play the situation itself is modern. *Yayati* is not glorified and Chitralekha's pain is underscored. She is victimized not only by Yayati but also by Pooru, who totally ignores her dreams and desires.

Through *Yayati's* myth Karnad brings to the fore the conflict between tradition and modernity, reason and emotions and also society and individual. The play makes some powerful statements by articulating "a set of values that I [Karnad] had been unable to arrive at rationally" (74). *Yayati*, thus, bears out the power of ancient myths to resolve some of the most complex dilemmas of the modern man.

Attacking Dogma and Hypocrisy: *The Fire and the Rain*

The Fire and the Rain is a telling proof of Karnad's brilliance and his ability to transform the Indian folklore , mythological tales and historical episodes into engaging plays. The play was originally written in Kannada as *Agni Mattu Male*, and then translated into English by the author himself. sThe play was commissioned by the prestigious Guthire Theatre, Minneapolis, U.S.A. and has been made into a motion picture, *Agni Varsha*.

The source of the play comes from the *Mahabharata*. It is an obscure story , with a play within a play, which centres around a fire sacrifice to bring rain. Karnad's play is a masterpiece. He depicts conflicting human emotions through his characters. It is an excellent combination of the elements—human, metaphysical and supernatural, that constitutes the core of the play.

The play is based upon 'The Myth of Yavakri' from the *Mahabharata*, a Sanskrit epic that consists of ancient legends and tales. This 'seemingly peripheral tale' of Yavakri is narrated by the ascetic Lomasha to the Pandavas as they wander across the land during their exile. It occurs in chapter 135-38 of the Vana Parva (Forest Canto) of the *Mahabharata*. Karnad came across the story of Yavakri and Paravasu in C.Rajagopalachari's abridged edition of the *Mahabharata*. Influenced by the mythological aspects of the tale, he decided to write a play on it. Karnad worked upon it for thirty-seven years and accorded it a complex form and structure, making it relevant to the present times. The metaphysical and spiritual legacy of the *Rigveda* and the *Mahabharata* is skilfully synthesized by Karnad as he blends the myth of Yavakri with some other archetypal myths of India.

Karnad employs several myths and legends, each having a standpoint of its own. All these viewpoints, however, refer to the central story. Karnad's disillusionment with dead and worn-out traditions is clearly discernible in the play. It is an outright condemnation of the dogma and hypocrisy associated with the orders of religion. Another point driven home through mythic references is the possibility of the annihilation of the cosmos itself if human vices rampant in society go unchecked.

The myth which forms the substance of the play is centered around a seven-year long fire sacrifice to appease the gods to send rain. It is through seduction, murder and betrayal that the tale reaches its climax which is as unexpected as it is philosophically resonant. Karnad presents a fabulous dramatic tale fusing together all human emotions , from deceit and betrayal to affection and revenge (Jacket, *The Fire and the Rain*).

The title of the play is notably important, Karnad juxtaposes two contrasting elements, the fire and the rain, which impel us to analyse the symbolic meanings widely associated with these motifs. Rain symbolises purification, fertility and growth. Fire on the contrary is associated with passion, fury, creative energy, law in nature and at times with consciousness and also with the passage of time and life. In the vedic tradition large number of hymns were addressed and related to Agni; also called the mystic fire. Agni has multiple meanings, "it means fire, aspiration, force of consciousness, an urge, mounting and burning askesis" (Joshi, 6). 'Agni' is also associated with the life-force which symbolizes true soul or psychic being. In his 'notes' to the play Karnad talks about the meaning and significance of the Kannada phrase '*Agni Mattu Male*'. He explains that 'Agni' is a Sanskrit word for fire and carries with it the connotations of holiness, of ritual status, of ceremony. " 'Agni' is what burns in sacrificial altars, acts as a witness at weddings and is lit at cremations ." 'Male' in Kannada means rain , pure , and simple, and 'Mattu' means 'and'. Karnad further adds:

Thus, the phrase, Agni Mattu Male, in addition to counterpointing two physical elements normally seen as antagonistic, also sets up several other oppositions: between an Indo-Aryan (Sanskrit) and a Dravidian (Kannada) language, between the Pan- Indic and the regional points of view, between the classical 'Marga' and the less exalted 'desi' traditions , between the elevated and the mundane (here one needs to tread cautiously) the sacred and the secular. (Karnad, *The Fire and the Rain*, 63)

The binary opposition between the fire and the rain in the play is clearly stated. The fire sacrifice by Paravasu to please Indra , the god of rains is at the core of the play. The play begins with a Prologue which introduces us to the drought ridden land where it "has not rained adequately for ten years" (1). Paravasu is the conducting priest whose responsibility is to see that "no errors of omission or commission" take place in the performance of the sacrifice. 'It is an impressive panorama' as there are many alters where priests are "offering oblations to the fire, while singing the prescribed hymns in unison" (1). Yajna has always been a significant part of the Vedic culture. Karnad too uses it as a central metaphor in his play. The conditional texts describe theatre as a yajna, which is said to be "a desirable fire sacrifice of the eyes". As Kalidasa puts it : "Kantam Kratum Chakshusham," meaning that which pleases the eyes.

The story of the play revolves around two characters –sages Bharadwaja and Raibhaya. While Raibhaya was a learned man who lived with his two sons, Paravasu and Aravasu, Bharadwaja concentrated on his ascetic practices. Yavakri, Bharadwaja's son felt that his father had not received the due respect and recognition. Instead of mortifying himself and practicing austerities, Yavakri, having obtained a boon of eternal knowledge from Lord Indra, now returns from ten years of meditation. He believes that Paravasu is unfit to be the high priest. Blind Raibhaya summons a demon, the Brahma Rakshasa, to kill Yavakri, who is guilty of upsetting the tranquillity of the region with his dissension. As Paravasu is in the last stages of his seven year old yajana, the play unfolds a love story between Aravasu and a tribal girl Nittilai. Aravasu is all set to defy his Brahmin order and visit the village and seek Nittilai's hand from her father in the presence of the panchayat.

Yavakri and Vishakha's relationship is yet another love story used by Karnad to make the play more powerful, particularly in the modern context. Vishakha is Paravasu's wife but it is revealed that she has been forced to marry him. She finds herself rejected by Paravasu and lusted after by Raibhaya, her father-in –law. The meeting between Yavakri and Vishakha rekindles old ties and Yavakri ends up seducing

Vishakha. Yavakri's misdemeanour infuriates Raibhaya and he invokes the 'Kritya' spirit and sends him to kill Yavakri.

One of the spirits invoked by Raibhya approaches Yavakri seductively in the form of Vishakha and steels the urn which contained water to make him immune to danger. She spills the sacred water that Yavakri carried with him. The spirit now transforms into a Rakshasa who chases him till death.

Yavakri runs towards the lake in search of water, but the lake dries up and not a drop is left to save him. Finally he tries to enter his father's hermitage, but a blind man who fails to recognize Yavakri does not let him enter. At that moment the Rakshasa kills Yavakri. When Bharadwaja learns that his son has been killed by the demon, he curses Raibhaya that he would die at the hands of his elder son. Later, on realising his folly in cursing a friend , he enters fire and immolates himself.

Paravasu and Aravasu conduct a fire sacrifice--- a yajna to persuade the gods Aravasu, on learning of the reunion of Yavakri and Vishakha , sneaks out of the yajna in the night and visits his home. Paravasu, the elder son of Raibhaya while returning home, through the forests, mistakes the black deer skin, which his father was wearing for a wild animal and unintentionally kills him, thus proving Raibhaya's curse to be true. On realising the blunder committed by him, he cremates his father and returns to the sacrificial enclosure. He says to Aravasu:

Since you are not capable of performing the sacrifice alone, go and perform the penitential rites prescribed for Brahminicide. I'll carry on with the sacrifice (35).

Aravasu obeys his brother and performs the last rites of their father. He fails to reach Nittilai's village in time, and her father gets her married to someone from the village. When Aravasu returns to the sacrificial enclosure, Paravasu blames him for killing their father and insults him. He turns to the King and says that this man is a Brahmin-killer and he should not be allowed to enter the sacrificial enclosure.

PARAVASU: What is he doing in these sanctified precincts? Throw him out-out! out! Demon! (38).

The King orders Aravasu to be thrown out of the Kingdom. Aravasu protests that he is innocent but to no use. He then decides to do penance to please the Sun god. Pleased by his prayers, the gods appear. Aravasu asks them to restore Yavakri to life along with Bharadwaja and Raibhaya, and make Paravasu forget his evil act. The gods grant him the boon and Yavakri is rebuked for his folly. Meanwhile Nittilai leaves her husband and rescues Aravasu and looks after him till he gains strength to act in the play.

In the beginning of the play we are told that a drama troupe has arrived in the town, pleading for an opportunity to put on a play that might also summon rain from the heavens. The Actor Manager tells Paravasu:

... if Indra is to be pleased and bring to an end this long draught which ravages our land a fire sacrifice is not enough. A play has to be performed along with it (34).

The performance of the play serves an important purpose in the play. The troupe has obtained permission from Paravasu to stage a play at the Yajana site in order to please Lord Indra. They require a lead actor and Aravasu decides to join them in the play.

The enactment of the play before Paravasu and the King is the finale. Aravasu plays the demon and the play turns into reality when he rushes to the yajna site and burns down the temple. Paravasu realizing that all is lost, enters the fire and is consumed by it. Nittilai is then killed by her brother and husband for dishonouring the village and family.

As Aravasu laments in grief with the body of Nittilai in his arms, god Indra appears and pleased with his enactment, grants him a boon of fulfilling his single wish. Although he could ask for rain , Aravasu wants Nittilai to come back to life. Indra says that such a wish would reverse time, and ultimately the same events would be repeated. The Brahma Rakshasa who killed Yavakri appears and begs Aravasu to liberate him. The demon convinces Aravasu that this is what Nittilai would have wanted. Aravasu then asks Indra to liberate the Brahmrakshasa. The play ends with the sky honouring the purity of love between Aravasu and Nittilai, and the long awaited rain finally blesses the land.

Thus, the play extends much beyond the tale from the *Mahabharata.* Karnad enlarges the scope of myths, by dramatising them the way no other dramatist has probably done. Karnad has projected the myth of Yavakri very effectively incorporating it in the main plot of the play . The other myth employed by Karnad is the slaying of the demon

Vritra by Indra, which is one of the archetypal myths of India. This myth is taken from the Rigveda and appears in the *Mahabharata* also with modifications.

The myth of Indra and Vrita as Karnad uses it, centres around Paravasu and Aravasu. This Vedic myth is an archetypal myth dealing with the Indian obsession with fratricide. This forms the sub-plot of the play.

Legends of the slaying of a serpent or dragon appear in many cultures. In Hindu mythology, one such story centres on god Indra and the "footless and handless" demon Vritra, described as both snake and dragon. The tale is told in the Vedas and dates back to the time when Indra was the king of gods. Using a divine thunderbolt, Indra struck Vritra between the shoulders, slicing open the mountain on which the demon lay. The blow separated heaven from earth and land from water. The waters that Vritra had contained flowed forth to bring life. Indra's heroic victory made him the champion of all who struggled to overcome obstacles or resistance.

In the *Rigveda* , 'the shoulderless one' (a serpent) swallows rivers and hides water inside him. Indra , by killing him, releases water and 'like lowing cows, the river flows out'. Indra is hailedas 'Vritrahan', who is the Hindu God of Rain. In the nineteenth century an interpretation was made of this myth that the release of water by the serpent signifies bringing down rain (Brokington, 11).

There is another myth associated with Indra. Frightened at the sight of the release of water by the snake, he fled like a falcon across ninety-nine rivers. In the *Mahabharata* the myth is presented in a different form, where Indra is shown having lost his central position in the Hindu Pantheon. The myth depicts Indra's treachery, in which he kills Vishvarupa (also called Trishiras, the three-headed one), son of Tvastri. Tvastri then gives birth to another son, Vritra, by a female demon, and tells him to kill Indra. Indra unable to overcome the new enemy has to resort to trickery to survive. Having killed Vritra, he suffers from the guilt of Brahminicide.

The Indra -Vrita myth is symbolic of a deep anxiety, which informs the whole of Indian mythology, the Indian obsession with fratricide, the fear of brother destroying brother . The epics of the *Ramayana* and the *Mahabharata* express another facet of this anxiety. In the *Ramayana* there is fraternal bonding between Rama and his brothers. However, the betrayals of Sugriva and Vibhishana mark the counterpoint. In the *Mahabharata* the bonding of brothers within the Pandavas and the Kuru clans is as strong as the enmity between the cousins is fierce and unrelenting.

The fire sacrifice which forms the integral part of the play is a hearty ritualistic ceremony. It was a rite of great importance during the Vedic times, and became an essential ceremony to be performed on any occasion. As noted earlier, Kalidasa talks of theatre as the 'desirable fire sacrifice of the eyes'. Thus, there is an unmistakable bond between the ritual of fire sacrifice and theatre.

The yajna was central in the Vedic era as a ceremonial rite. The sophisticated symbolism and magic of the yajna contrasted with the simplified aestheticism of the puja, as the personal message of the former, performed for the particular donor (yajamana), contrasted with the public character of the latter –a rite dedicated to a god in the name of all worshippers. (Lidovo,6)

Kireet Joshi defines sacrifice as an important symbol of the vedic tradition and knowledge. He says:

Sacrifice or yajna symbolises inner submission, consecration and surrender to higher powers, gods and the Supreme. Outwardly, this submission was translated into an elaborate ritual of collecting sacrificial materials, lighting them in order to kindle the sacrificial fire and offering… butter, grains and other materials (Joshi, 90).

The entire act of performing a sacrifice was accompanied by recitation of hymns and mantras and often marked by appropriate hand movements, gestures and mudras. Thus, a close connection was established between the words, the ideas and reality. "It was against this background that the ritual of yajna was perfected in great detail and… great attention was paid to the performance of sacrifice" (Joshi, 90).

In terms of both origin and practice theatrical performance complements Vedic ritual and has a place within it. In the Notes to the play Karnad "argues pointedly that theatre as theorized and practiced in antiquity is not the 'secular' counterpoint to a yajna but a parallel performance that can even offer a welcome diversion from the rigours of ritual" (Dharwadker, Vol. 2, xix). Dharwadker aptly remarks that *The Fire and the Rain* is Karnad's "most ambitiously metatheatrical play, one in which performance is not just a framing device but a thematic preoccupation and an intrinsic part of the main action" (xx). In the broadest sense, Agni Mattu Male is a drama of sacrifice and expiation.

The Fire and the Rain opens with a fire sacrifice designed to appease gods to send rain. In a similar vein, *The Mahabharata* opens with a sacrifice that was to go on for twelve years. The intervals between the ritual acts were used for narrating tales. The spare time was also devoted to the performance of plays. The whole of the Mahabharata was narrated during such intervals between rites. In the play, *The Fire and The Rain*, Karnad follows the same tradition and narrates the mythical stories in the course of the play . The performance by the drama troupe conforms to the ritualistic pattern.

The mythical Brahma Rakshasa or a demon plays an important role in the play. We are told in the 'Prologue' that it is a Brahmin's soul trapped in limbo between death and rebirth. He moves around the sacrificial precincts, though no human eye can see him. He expresses his agony and desire of release from this state to Paravasu:

BRAHMA RAKSHASA: ...A soul trapped in nothingness like a foetus stitched up inside its mother's sac. You can't imagine the horror of that existence... Free me from this pain. Liberate me I want to fade away. To become nothing (36).

Raibhaya, Paravasu's father had called him back in time to kill Yavakri and now as Paravasu has killed his father, the

Brahma Rakshasa has become a lost soul. Being an evil spirit, he is barred entry into the sacrificial enclosures. It is only Paravasu who can liberate his soul, but Paravasu laughs and says:

PARAVASU: (Laughs) Yavakri asked for 'all knowledge' in a begging bowl. You ask for the final release. Moksha! The demands seems to be escalating! I am not interested in your final release. I am not even interested in my final release. (Mocking) 'Liberate' you! How's one supposed to do that? (36).

The only way by which the Brahma Rakshasa can be released is by pleading before the gods through Paravasu, who denies him any kind of help. In the end it is Aravasu only who finally helps in the liberation of the demonic soul.

Karnad has employed this myth very interestingly. The myth also reminds us about the Kalachakra, by which the past can be reversed or dead people can be called back to life. The Actor-Manager acts as the Bhagavata of the play who tells us that he had made a perfect choice for this fire sacrifice. The play to be enacted is about "The Triumph of Lord Indra. A play about the struggle between Lord Indra and the demon Vritra"(Karnad,50).

Aravasu is assigned to play the role of Vritra as he loves the ghoulish make-up, the roaring and thumping and the acrobatics. Nittilai reveals her happiness and says that she is happy that Aravasu is not playing the role of Indra. The Actor-Manager enters with the costumes and the mask of Vritra. The mask has been used very effectively to lend immense power to the play. The Actor- Manager as Karnad's spokesman, talks about the significance of masks .

ACTOR MANAGER: This is the mask of Vritra the demon... Surrender and pour life into it. But remember, once you bring a mask to life you have to keep a tight control over it, otherwise, it'll try to take over. (52).

He cautions the actor who has to wear the mask and tells him the proper way of using it:

It'll begin to dictate terms to you and you must never let that happen. Prostrate yourself before it. Pray to it. Enter it. Then control it.(52)

The Epilogue enhances the importance of Indra- Vritra myth as the play within the play begins with Aravasu dancing violently. The lore of Indra and Vishwarupa, the King of Men as mentioned earlier deals with the killing of Vishwarupa by Indra deceptively. Indra was the King of Gods and considered himself to be Supreme in the Three Worlds. He was unrivalled till his brother acquired great wisdom and gentleness. Indra felt like an 'eclipsed moon' and he decided to destroy him. Indra's father had a third son, a demon, Vritra , King of the Nether World. Indra wanted to isolate Vishwarupa with intentions to kill him and he organized a fire sacrifice in honour of his father Brahma, the lord of All Creation.

Vishwarupa was invited by Indra to attend the sacrifice. Vritra , who accompanied Vishwarupa was not permitted by Indra to enter the sacrificial precincts as his mother was a demon so a demon's blood flowed in his veins. In the play, when questioned by Vishwarupa, Indra replies, " The rules are more ancient than us. We cannot tamper with them" (54).

So treacherously Indra asks Vishwarupa to enter the sacrificial pavilion, while he is seated near the altar to offer oblations to the gods. As soon as Vishwarupa enters the pavilion with his back towards Indra, Indra plunges a thunderbolt into Vishwarupa's back. This incident has a strong parallel with *The Fire and The Rain*. Paravasu has treacherously blamed Aravasu of killing their father , whereas Paravasu himself has killed him.

On the other hand, Vritra hears the bewailing cry of Vishwarupa and in a violent frenzy attacks Indra. Aravasu playing Vritra rushes into the real sacrificial pavilion, where Paravasu was conducting rites. The Actor-Manager realises what has happened.

Actor-Manager: It's the mask – it is the mask come alive. Restrain him or there will be chaos (57).

Aravasu has turned into a Vritra who flies in the smoke like a Rakshasa and disappears in the flames. The Brahmins call it a 'doomsday' as the tribals and the savages are eating and drinking the food kept for the gods. Aravasu burns the sacrificial enclosure and the fire reduces everything to ashes. Ironically the fire sacrifice which was intended to please the god of Rain , brings fire instead of rain, destroying everything.

Nittilai died 'like a sacrificial animal', Paravasu 'walks into the blazing enclosure', and Aravasu stands inside the burning structure. Suddenly, "the entire atmosphere gets an ethereal hue the voice of Indra is heard from the skies" (59).

Pleased by Aravasu he grants him a wish by which he liberates the Brahma Rakshasa. The play ends with blowing winds, lightning and thunder accompanied by rain.

The myths weave an intricate pattern in *The Fire and the Rain*, making it more complex and richer. Karnad, however, does not employ mythological framework for its own sake. He uses myths to highlight certain concerns which are intrinsically modern in spirit. The play is an important statement vis a vis the uselessness of orthodox practices. At the same time, it conveys a message about the purity of true love. It is the love of Nittilai and Aravasu that finally brings rain to a parched land, where debauchery was rampant. *The Fire and The Rain*, bears out the eternal significance of myths.

Bali: The Sacrifice

Every aspect of life in India is associated with religion. Intertwined with religion are many rituals and superstitions. "Forming a part of the cultural identity of India, religion shapes and constructs the distinct identity of the individual". Religion and ritual form an integral part of Karnad's plays also. The two are interwoven into the fabric of the texts in a way that they bring forth the mythic and ritualistic correlation. Karnad employs the ritualistic myths for the dramatic representation of various themes.

Karnad's *Bali: The Sacrifice* is yet another play in which he has drawn upon the thirteenth-century Kannada epic,

Yashodara Charite, by Janna. This epic in turn refers back to an eleventh-century Sanskrit epic by Vadiraja, which again has a cross reference to the ninth-century Sanskrit epic, *Yashastilaka*, by Somadeva Suri. The plot of *Yashatilaka* centres on the conflicting ideologies represented by the queen and the queen mother. The queen mother is the unrelenting Shaktapati; the Kali-worshipper who considers ritualistic violence an important part of a sacrifice, whereas the queen being a follower of Jainism rejects violence.

Karnad first came across the myth of the cock of Dough, in his teens and later developed it into a play. He remarks that the myth continued to reveal unexpected meanings with passing years and he is glad he deferred employing it in the play. He wrote *Bali: The Sacrifice* when the Leicester Haymarket Theatre commissioned him to write for them. The play was first presented at Leicester on 31 May 2002.

Bali: The Sacrifice is a bold statement on the philosophy of violence and religious tolerance. However, parallel to this runs the theme of assertion of desire and acknowledgement of how elusive happiness can be in a materialistic world. The play is unique in many ways. Drawing on myth to interrogate violence associated with rituals, it brings into focus the public and the personal domains. Karnad highlights the idea that intended violence is as wicked as the actual violence. By foregrounding the myth of the Cock of Dough, the playwright emphasizes the way man's innate violence and brutal intentions are sometimes masked under the veneer of ritualistic actions.

The play, *Bali: The Sacrifice* enacts the story of King Yasudha who has converted to his wife's religion, Jainism, the sect which emphasises non-violence. One night the queen is entranced by a sonorous voice coming from a ruined temple. The singer is the Mahout that is the King's elephant keeper, who turns out to be a hunchback with a scarred face and a limp. Seduced by the voice, the queen surrenders herself physically to the Mahout. The King follows her to the temple and his mother also comes after him. The King invents a dream as a cover-up to hide the queen's infidelity.

The queen mother interprets the dream as ominous and declares that a hundred sheep be sacrificed to propitiate the goddess Kali. The queen Amritamati who is a staunch Jain, revolts at the idea of conducting a sacrifice saying that since the dream did not occur the sacrifice is unnecessary. The King is, thus, in a dilemma, because of his allegiance to Jainism. To resolve the issue the queen mother brings the cock of dough as a substitute for a hundred sheep. The King is in a fix as the intention behind the killing is as crucial as is the actual violence. He is 'in a claustrophobic no-escape situation' (Asnani, 20). The queen believes that there is a way out. She says what happened in the temple was immaterial, and was a moment of ecstasy. Of course, she broke all conventions when she fantasized about that man, but she does not consider it as a matter of infidelity. She promises that she will not visit the temple again.

The play takes up the issue of violence, a topic which has been in debate for centuries. In the preface to the play Karnad remarks that 'it is a tribute to the astuteness and sensitivity of Mahatma Gandhi who clearly imbibed the importance of non-violence for the growth and development of India. Tracing back the history of vedic sacrifices Karnad reminds us of the sacrifices conducted by Brahmin priests, which involved the slaughter of animals as offerings to the gods. The Jains were antagonistic to this view and believed that indulging in any kind of violence whether minor or accidental meant 'forfeiting one's moral status as a human being' (Karnad, Two Plays, 69). Later the Brahmins renounced blood sacrifice and miniature figurines, made of dough, were substituted for living animals. The Jains argued that this was no solution as even if no animals were slaughtered the figures of dough carried within them the original violent impulse. The choice of dough has another ritual associated with it. An offering makes sense only if it is meant as food for gods. However, the dough is cooked and consumed by the devotees.

Jainism held that the priests simply substituted actual violence with violence in intention which was equally dehumanizing. The debate thus raised questions like, if one is condemning actual violence and indulging in intended violence, is he not shutting himself up in 'solipsistic world, a bleak, guilt-ridden, existence with no hope of absolution?' (70). The moral responsibility that one holds for merely intending to commit an act that one has not actually carried out in real life, brings in the complexity in a ritualistic and ethical act.

Karnad emphasizes the multiple roles played by various legends in Indian culture and acknowledges the view point of Professor Bimal Krishna Matilal, who pointed out:

Great epics, apart from being the source of everything else, constitute an important component of what we may term as moral philosophical thinking of the Indian tradition… The tradition itself was very self-conscious about moral values, moral conflicts and dilemmas, as well as difficulties of what we call practical reason or practical wisdom. The consciousness found its expression in the epic stories and narrative literature. (70)

It is this 'self-consciousness' that has found voice in Karnad's play *Bali: The Sacrifice.* The play begins with a song sung by the queen which serves as a prologue to the play.

As the world is divided

into two orbs:

One lit up by the sun

the other hid in the shade.

So also the human soul, …

is split into two realms –

one of the spirits that adore

the blood and gore

of the bright, shining blade…

and the other

ruled by the spirits that bid

you pause…

lest you harm a life. (73)

The song brings out the element of dual forces that exist and govern the human beings. In the play this duality is represented by the two main characters; the queen mother and the queen Amritamati. In contrast the King's song reflects his agony, anguish and perplexity. The sexual undertones and the projection of the queen as if she is in a trap that she cannot escape are evident in the song:

So we begin our tale-

and in the tale

the King and the Queen…

- she on his lap

become half his royal frame

or entwined in bed, tangled together

they must turn

into a four-armed deity…

for the good of the land.

But

woe betide the times

where the King sits alone

outside on the steps

racked by sighs

while the Queen cannot

escape her lover's thighs. (74)

Girish Karnad has incorporated songs to comment on the play in the manner of a 'Sutradhar'. At other places, they indicate the passage of time bringing back memories of the days gone by. The first song refers powerfully to the queen's distaste for violence and also her disillusionment with those "that adore the blood and gore..." The second song underscores two important issues – the first associated with the Queen being trapped in a situation, she was instinctually drawn to, the second dealing with the King's anguish and helplessness.

Girish Karnad deals with some pertinent issues of the modern age through *Bali*. The play is a reflection on traditional moral codes and their validity. By foregrounding such issues as adultery and transgression, the playwright invites us to delve into the complexities of morality and its comprehension vis-à-vis the strict moral codes of society. The queen apparently has committed an act, which will never have moral sanction. The play, however, seems to question the validity of moral codes that society creates and imposes, completely disregarding an individual's personal perception. The play takes into account the fact that the queen allows herself to be charmed by a low-born and subsequently surrenders herself to him. But she never regrets those moments, not even when she is confronted by the King. Her love for the king makes her resolute not to reveal her identity to Mahout even as she maintains she values the beautiful moments spent with him.

Karnad endows the queen with remarkable self-assuredness and courage. She is committed to the idea of non-violence throughout the play. She loves the king but is disillusioned with his weak willed persona. Though he has converted to Jainism, he succumbs to his mother's dictates to perform a mock sacrifice. For the Queen, the intended violence is as condemnable as the actual act of violence. Horrified at the prospect of the killing of the cock of Dough, which is almost like a real cock to her, she prefers to sacrifice herself, exemplifying courage of conviction.

The queen is outraged when Mahout gives the king tips on lovemaking and king actually begins to follow him asking him about her 'vulnerable' and 'erogenous' zones. She retorts, "I'm not a piece of meat for you to pick and paw at" (117).

In spite of turning the conventional standards of morality topsy turvey, Karnad establishes the moral superiority of the queen, who is more admirable than the King, who lusts after her and even the Mahout, who shows insensitivity in hurting her. The queen is certainly not lustful, she simply looks for emotional and spiritual solace that Mahout's song provided her and she let herself go.

The moral bankruptcy of the king becomes apparent when he tells a bewildered queen that her miscarriage was the result of their not listening to the Mother's wishes to sacrifice animals. The queen is horrified:

Queen:So I lost my baby because I didn't follow your mother's orders? Because I didn't kill and maim?

King:I am not saying that.

Queen:Yes, you are. Late in my life, I become pregnant and I have a miscarriage – and you are saying that was a punishment meted out to me for my defiance. (113)

Karnad's play reveals how forthright and honest the queen is. She does not hide anything from the King, though she admits it was not her intention to hurt him and that she wants to come back to him. However, she would certainly not carry out the ritual of killing a Cock of Dough:

Queen:I want to come back to you. I feel fuller. Richer. Warmer. But not ashamed. Because I didn't plan it. It happened. And it was beautiful. (A long pause. He stares at her). I'm sorry. If this rite is going to blot the moment out, that would be the real betrayal. I'll do anything else. (119)

The queen evokes the readers' admiration in spite of her act of surrender to the Mahout. However, the king comes across as a spineless being who is carried away easily. The queen is steadfast and shows strong commitment to the ideal of non-violence, whereas the King shows an infirm disposition.

The assertion by the queen of her non-violence and acknowledgement of her sexuality obviously subvert the authoritative order of status and gender. In somewhat the same manner Mahout also emerges as the agent of subversion of the traditional power structures. As if this is not enough, the appearance of the King at the wrong time makes the queen exclaim.

Queen:Why did you come here?

(Pause)

Why did you? Until he saw you –

King:I'm concerned about you. You about him.

Queen:I'm talking about us both.

(Pause)

Until he saw you, he didn't know who I was. I was just a woman, any woman. Now he can gloat.

King(Spits out Contemptuously): Him!

Queen:No, me. For one night, I was nameless. (87-88)

Even the queen finds her authority being eroded as the private domain spills over the public. *Bali: The Sacrifice* deals with a story, remote in time and place. However, the issues it brings to the surface, are steeped in modernity. This play bears out that Karnad's drama has tremendous relevance to contemporary reality.

Chapter-3
Representing Modernity through Folk and Theatre

The folk theatre emerged out of the oral tradition of story-telling. In the early stages of its development it was purely devotional and revolved around religion, local legends and mythology. With the passage of time the term acquired new meanings, it came to be associated with the folk stories of romance and valour and biographical accounts of local heroes. The Indian folk theatre can be broadly classified into two categories - religious and secular. These two forms exist simultaneously, one influencing the other. The folk and traditional theatre forms are mainly narrative or vocal, that is, singing and recitation based, like Ramlila, Rasleela, Bhand, Nautanki, Yakshagana, Jatra and Svang.

Every folk form has a theatrical style of its own and each differs from the other in execution, staging and acting style. The folk or the traditional theatre that evolved out of rural roots was closer to the rural Svang. The roots movement has close affinity with the traditional 'folk' forms of Indian theatre. In their search for an indigenous modern Indian theatre, the roots playwrights revived the cultural folk forms of story-telling and folk theatre to resist the colonial culture. Mulk Raj Anand in his book *The Indian Theatre* defines

Indian theatre in terms of folk theatre. He asserts the importance of the folk forms in the development of modern Indian theatre and emphasises that the knowledge of the traditional folk theatre should be acquired to formulate a new indigenous tradition of the Indian theatre. Shanta Gandhi, one of the founding members of the Indian People's Theatre Association (IPTA), makes a significant remark in this context. She says:

Every age has necessarily to reinterpret its inheritance in light of its own contemporary reality in order to make it meaningful, rather than carry the dead weight of history. (Gandhi, 14)

The roots movement seeks to dissociate itself from the vestiges of the colonial theatre and align itself with the folk forms. There were attempts during the colonial times to push to periphery the indigenous theatre forms such as 'Jatra' in Bengal and 'Nautanki' in Maharashtra. As theatre became anglicized, the educated upper classes began to disparage the immensely popular Jatra. Similarly, the performances of 'Nautanki' style plays were found crude by "English-educated Indian audience schooled in Shakespeare" (Mee, 51).

While colonial theatre continued to be used as a model for many productions, some conscious attempts were also made by playwrights to challenge colonial values while using the western dramaturgy. At the same time a divide between the text-based drama and performance based genres such as Jatra and Tamasha became apparent. This was a consequence of the colonial agenda.

Gradually, however, the playwrights realized that the tastes of the audiences in India differed from those of the audiences in Europe. As a result, many plays written in western idiom were presented in collaboration with companies that promoted performance based theatre forms, such as Jatra, Tamasha and Nautanki. This new theatre form came to be called hybrid theatre. As Erin B. Mee puts it:

Once 'high culture' was equated with literature and colonial culture, and 'rural performance' was equated with an 'authentic', 'Indian' culture and, rural performance was 'rediscovered' by nationalists and used for political and social purposes in the late nineteenth and early twentieth centuries. This renewed interest in 'folk performance', and its specific use as a tool to fight colonial culture, paved the way for the roots movements. (Mee, 67)

The playwrights belonging to the 'roots' movement, were inspired by the indigenous theatre. Their own quest for identity led them to rediscover the power of folk forms. Girish Karnad acknowledges the versatility of the Indian folk theatre tradition and draws upon the "style and form of the theatre which is closer to the consciousness of people, consistent with our cultural traditions... yet aesthetically satisfying' (Goel, 204).

Folk theatre strategies are employed by Karnad as thematic and technical devices to convey his ideas. He employs the conventions of folk tales or story telling and motifs of folk theatre that is, masks, curtains, mime, songs, the commentator-narrator or the sutradhar, dolls, horse-man and the story within a story. Karnad incorporates the rich resources of the native folk theatre, such as, Nautanki and other folk forms as well. He combines these techniques with the western dramaturgies to successfully create what has come to be known as hybrid theatre.

Hayavadana: Blending the Folk and the Western dramaturgies

When Girish Karnad's *Hayavadana* was published in 1971, it was hailed as a classic example of the roots movement. Suresh Awasthi "credited Karnad with having evolved 'a new dramatic form' and singled out *Hayavadana* as an example of what could be done creatively with 'folk forms' in an urban setting" (SNA 1971: 5, 29). *Hayavadana,* thus, was a landmark play that was a conscious attempt "to create a hybrid theatre that reflects the complex subjectivities of post-independence reality" (Mee, 142). Karnad weaves together in *Hayavadana,* the eastern, and the western dramaturgies, creating "a hybrid dramaturgical structure, acting style and visual practice that offer spectators a model for practising cultural ambidexterity—the ability to successfully and easily operate simultaneously in two or more cultural systems without privileging either one" (Dharwadkar 1997: 108-33).

Fig. II: The Ganesha puja at the opening of *Hayavadana*.

Source: Sangeet Natak Akademi, New Delhi.

In *Hayavadana*, Karnad projects the myth of Ganesha who, being an "embodiment of imperfection of incompleteness" is worshipped as "the destroyer of incompleteness" (Karnad, 1). *Hayanadana* is amongst the most widely acknowledged plays of Girish Karnad. The play won the Natya Sangh award for the best play of 1971. Written in 1970 and later translated into English by the author himself, *Hayavadana* articulates the imaginative richness of Indian myths and folklore in their myriad colours and profound meanings. The mythological and folk legends are blended so as to bring to the fore the theme of universal quest for perfection and completeness. The play is 'a riddling philosophical thriller' in which Karnad problematises the issues of personal identity" (Chatterji, 1). The theme of incompleteness runs throughout the play. Karnad therefore, presents Indian myths associated with Lord Ganesha as archetypes.

Karnad makes use of the native folk-theatre 'Yakshagana' and other folk-forms with great deftness. He weaves into the play the myth of half- horse and half-man, *Hayavadana*, who hovers between being man and god in search of fulfilment in an imperfect world. The body and intellect divide also occurs as a major theme in the play.

Regarding the subject of the play, Karnad states in his 'Notes' to the play that "The central episode in the play—the story of Devadatta and Kapila is based on a tale from the *Vetalpanchavimshika*, but I have drawn heavily on Thomas Mann's reworking of the tale in *The Transposed Heads* ..."(Karnad, Notes). Erin B. Mee observes:

The transposition of heads constitutes the main crux of the play, which results in a confusion of identities revealing the essential ambiguity of human nature. Hayavadana's *origins are intergeneric (a folktale transformed into a novella into a play) and intercultural (the story travelled from India to Germany and back again). Tnter-ness' pervades* Hayavadana *at every level, from its origins to its thematic content to its production history. (Mee, 143)*

In the *Kathasaritasagara*, this head-body split occurs between body and soul; in Mann's novella the dichotomy is between intellect and emotion; in Karnad's play the conflict is between self and other.

In Thomas Mann's version of the story, he argues and ridicules the philosophy which holds the head superior to the body. He considers the human body a fit instrument for the fulfilment of human destiny. The original version of Mann's story poses a moral problem and uses it to ridicule the mechanical conception of life, which differentiates between body and soul. Similarly, in *Hayavadana*, Karnad's intention is to satirize the body-soul divide in modern life quite like Thomas Mann.

The *Vetalpanchavimshika* and Somdeva's *Brihatkathasaritsagar* also refer to the same tale of the transposition of heads. In the Vetala story the problem was solved by King Vikram, but in Karnad's play *Hayavadana*,, the real problem begins from the point where the Vetala story ends. The plot of the play is based on folk literature as well as legends from mythology. Devadatta, an accomplished Brahmin falls in love with a beautiful and intelligent girl Padmini. Devadatta's friend Kapila, son of an ironsmith succeeds in arranging their marriage. He is extremely devoted to his friend Devadatta for his wisdom. In course of time, however, Padmini gets attracted towards Kapila who is strong and virile.

Similarly, Kapila also admires her beauty. While on the their journey to Ujjain which Devadatta takes on the insistence of Padmini, he decides to sacrifice his head to goddess Kali, apparently in accordance with his earlier vow, but the fact is that he is unable to cope with the pangs of jealousy. When Kapila discovers the dead body of Devdatta, he too sacrifices his head ostensibly out of love for his friend. Padmini while searching for two stumbles upon their bodies and prays to goddess Kah to bring them back to life. The goddess asks her to put their heads back on their bodies. Padmini, however, transposes their heads with the result that there are two men now, one with Devadatta's head and another with Devadatta's body.

Since head is supposed to be superior to the body, the man with Devadatta's head wins over Kapila in being Padmini's husband. Ironically, this is also the opportunity for Padmini to have the best of two men, that is, Devadatta's head and Kapila's body. Kapila feels cheated but remains in the forest trying to strengthen and shape the Brahmin's body below his head. Padmini once again deceives her husband after the strong body of Kapila attached to Devadatta's head loses its original vigour. Walking into the embrace of Kapha, the child that she carries is claimed by her to be the child of both Kapila and Devadatta. The friends once again fight and are killed by each other.

The child who is associated with the myth of Hayavadana which is the basis of the sub-plot of the play, in fact adds to the significance of main theme of incompleteness and the quest for completeness. He can actually be identified with the myth of Hayavadana. A traveller takes him to his grandparents, where he is discovered to be unable to laugh like a human child. He laughs only when the horse-man born out of the union of a stallion (who in fact is gandharva cursed to live like a horse) and a Princess, laughs. Hayavadana is projected as a man with the head of a horse: 'haya' means horse and 'vadana' means face. Karnad has invested the title of the play with the idea of imperfection and ambiguity. The character of Hayavadana is invented as an example of 'incompleteness' which further gains significance as other related themes unfold in the course of the play.

In accordance with the Brechtian theatre, Karnad opens the play with the Bhagavata, the Sutradhar or commentator who directly talks to the audience and narrates what he sees. The Bhagavata keeps updating the audience about the happenings while commenting upon every situation in the play. The play opens with the projection of the myth of Ganesha, which like the other legends incorporated in the play, is associated with the motif of transposition of heads. Similarly the idea of imperfection and incompleteness is also related to this myth. Ironically, however, this God who is both imperfect and incomplete is worshipped as 'the destroyer of incompleteness'.

Lord Ganesha is worshipped at the beginning of traditional performance genres like *Yakshagana* by the performers as well as the spectators. Karnad incorporates it as a Hindu ritualistic element in *Hayavadana* where "to 'see' Ganesha as a deity in the context of a ritual is to receive darshan" (Mee, 159). The concept of 'darshan' refers to the visual contact between devotee and deity. The deity presents himself to be seen and the devotee sees or beholds the divine image to seek blessings. "In darshan, human sight mixes with divine insight to dispel maya, or illusion" (Babb, 398). Karnad introduces the image of Lord Ganesha onstage for the audiences to apprehend the theatrical performance as a real ritual. This involves the 'complex seeing' as practised by Brecht where the spectator perceives the image of Ganesha in multi-dimensional roles. The deity is seen as a mythological figure who prefigures as character in stories and plays, or as personified character - the Mangalmurti Viganharta, or as a representative of the Indian folk tradition. The invocation of Ganesha at the beginning of any work is significant. This form of multiple viewing is what cultural critic Henry Jenkins refers to as 'double viewing', which happens when a spectator 'sees' from several perspectives at once or simultaneously perceives many realities (173). 'The deity Ganesha is an exemplar, survivor of the head-body divide. The divided self as projected by *Hayavadana* in the play is used as "a metaphor for cultural difference, Ganesha challenges the production and promotion of cultural difference as both a source/sign of colonial authority and a source/sign of Indian national culture" (Mee, 145).

Keeping, in mind the mythic framework of the play, Karnad gives it a ritualistic opening. As the play begins, a mask of Ganesha is brought on the stage and kept on the chair. The Bhagavata sings verses in praise of 'Vakratunda Mahakaya' with the crooked face and distorted body, who is the lord and master of success and perfection. Lord Ganesha occupies a prime position among all Hindu Gods, he is one of the five prime Hindu deities Brahma, Vishnu, Shiva and Durga being the other four. Lord Ganesha has an elephantine countenance with a curved trunk, big ears and huge pot-bellied body of human being. He is believed to be the lord of success and destroyer of evils and obstacles. He is also worshipped as the god of education, knowledge, wisdom and wealth. Karnad would have his audiences believe that like all good things, his play too should invoke the blessings of Ganesha to have a smooth run free from obstacles.

O Elephant-headed Heramba whose flag is victory and who shines like a thousand suns.

O husband of Riddhi and Siddhi, seated on a mouse and decorated with a snake.

O single-tusked destroyer of incompleteness, we pay homage to you and start our play. (1)

As single-tusked or Ekadavta, the Lord has limitless powers. As Heramba, he removes obstacles. As Lambodara, he protects all worlds. As Surpa karma, he shows compassion by giving knowledge. These all are the names for Lord Vinayaka, who is the Lord of all. Lord Ganesha has four hands. In one hand he has a rope while in another he has an axe. With the axe he cuts off the attachment of his devotees to the world of plurality and thus ends all the sorrows that go with it. Ganpati is the embodiment of Buddhi and Janana (Wisdom). Truth emerges out of wisdom and ultimately leads to Ananda (bliss). This is the teaching of Ganapati.

In *Yakshagana,* which is a popular genre of dance drama performance in Karnataka, the Bhagavata is a central figure known as the 'director' or 'stage manager' who remains onstage and tells stories about lord Vishnu and his several incarnations. The Bhagavata is similar to the sutradhara of Sanskrit drama, who begins the play by introducing the frame story and the play to the audience. In Karnad's *Hayavadana:*

Bhagavata's dialogue is scripted but it is written so that it both seems improvised and has the sensibility of improvisation, referencing and valorizing oral storytelling practices that were negated by the colonial culture's privileging of written text... Bhagavata is a skilled practitioner of theatrical and cultural ambidexterity. (Mee, 167)

In *Hayavadana*, the opening speech by Bhagavata introduces us to the main theme of the play.

May Vighneshwara, the destroyers of obstacles, who removes all hurdles and crowns all endeavors with success, bless our performance now...An elephant's head on a human body, a broken tusk and a cracked belly - whichever way you look at him he seems the embodiment of imperfection, of incompleteness. How indeed can one fathom the mystery... [of] this very Vakratunda -Mahakaya... (1)

The Bhagavata speculates that it is not easy to unravel the mystery of this divine being. He is perplexed at the thought, that the Vighneshwara who is invoked by the Hindus, prior to any religious or auspicious ceremony to remove all obstacles though incomplete in himself, is the God who confers perfection. The impossibility of comprehending the significance of Ganesha is also stated by the Bhagavata:

Could it be that this Image of Purity and Holiness, this Mangalamoorty, intends to signify by his very appearance that the completeness of God is something no poor mortal can comprehend? (1)

The myth which centres on this crooked face and distorted body is related to Lord Shiva and Parvati. According to the legend, Lord Ganesha was created by goddess Parvati, wife of Lord Shiva. Parvati created Ganesha out of the sandalwood paste that she used for her bath and breathed life into him. Letting him stand guard at the door she went to have her bath. While Parvati was taking her bath Lord Shiva happened to come there and as Ganesha did not know him, he did not allow Lord Shiva to enter. Annoyed at this Lord Shiva beheaded his own child unknowingly. When Parvati cleared up the situation to Lord Shiva, she requested him to restore Ganesha to life. He immediately sent his 'ganas' to take the head of any living creature, whose mother was sleeping with her back towards her child. They found an elephant mother sleeping like this. The 'ganas' cut off the head of the baby elephant and put it on the body of Ganesha. In this way, Lord Ganesha acquired the image of the elephant-headed God.

In this connection, the Bhagavata makes a significant remark. He states:

It is not for us to understand this mystery or try to unravel it. Nor is it within our powers to do so. Our duty is merely to pay homage to the Elephant-headed god and get on with our play. (1)

Karnad 'recontextualizes' (Mee, 149) the elements of traditional performance so that the spectators can re-examine their theatrical experiences. Hayavadana's entrance is modelled on the traditional introductory dance form called *oddolaga* of the *Yakshagana*. The *oddolaga* introduces the audience with the epic characters by commenting upon their moral nature and the character is then blended with the story. In *Hayavadana* the Bhagavata introduces Hayavadana in the same manner by posing a series of questions. The question and answer section is also a borrowing from the *Yakshagana.*

The story within the story starts when the Bhagavata narrates the story in the manner of a folk tale, "This is the city of Dharamapura ruled by kind Dharamasheela whose fame and empire have already reached the ends of the eight directions. Two youths who dwell in this city are our heroes"(Karnad, Hayavadana, 1) He then introduces us to Devadatta and Kapila who are thes closest of friends-'one mind one heart' as the Bhagavata describes them. As observed earlier Devadatta is a man of intellect, Kapila a 'man of the body'. The people of Dharamasheela wonder at their friendship.

The Bhagavata's narration is interrupted by a Nata (Actor) who informs the Sutradhar that he has met a talking horse. This is Hayavadana, who has a man's body but a horse's head. He is sitting on the floor hiding his head between his knees. All his life he has been trying to get rid of his head and become a complete man. The Bhagavata, taking the horse's head for Hayavadana's mask tries to pull it off from his body with the help of one of his actors, 'Hayavadana offers no resistance, but can't help moaning when the pain becomes unbearable'. The truth dawns on the Bhagavata and he says 'Nata, this isn't a mask! It's his real head' (6).

Fig. III: Hayavadana with a horse's head.

Source: Sangeet Natak Akademi, New Delhi.

Hayavadana then tells the Bhagavata that he was born with it and relates the whole story of his birth. Karnad uses this myth very effectively. He makes the mythic character his own mouthpiece, who narrates his story most poignantly. The myth of Hayavadana goes on thus:

His mother was the beautiful Princess of Karnataka. Many suitors were invited by her father so that she could choose her own husband. Among them was the Prince of Araby, 'My mother took one look at that handsome prince sitting on his great white stallion- and she fainted'. (8)

To the utter surprise of everyone she said that she would only marry that horse and not the Prince. No one could dissuade her and she was ultimately married off to the white stallion. They spent fifteen years of their life together.

One morning she wakes up and no horse! In its place stood a beautiful celestial Being, gandharva. Apparently this celestial

Being had been cursed by the god Kuvera to be born a horse for some act of misbehaviour. After fifteen years of human tone he had become his original self again. (8)

Hayavadana in the play faces a similar identity crisis and is in search of completeness for which he has tried everything. And helplessly he asks Bhagavata if he could help him to become a complete man.

Karnad's treatment of the mythological legends is certainly loaded with meaning. However, his sarcastic intent puts these myths and the worn out conventions associated with them on trial. While the myth of Hayavadana is unfolded, one learns that in search of completeness, he has been to several places of pilgrimage and consulted innumerable fakirs and saints. Yet all this has been a meaningless pursuit. Karnad clearly seems to ridicule the mindless exercise of this kind for wish fulfilment. This is evident in the way the Bhagavata and the actor ask him questions;

BHAGAVATA: Banaras?

HAYAVADANA: What?

BHAGAVATA: If you go to Banaras and make a vow in front of the god there (9)

HAYAVADANA: I have tried that, didn't work .....Banaras,

Ramashevar Gokarm, Haridwar, Gaya, Kedarnath not only those but the Dargah of Khwaja Yusuf Baba, the Grotto of our Virgin Mary - I've tried them all. Magicians, mendicants, maharishis, fakirs saints and sadhus—sadhus with short hair... Sadhus in saffron-hanging, singing, rotating, gyrating - on the spikes, in the air... I've covered them all. (9)

In spite of all this he could not get rid of his horse head and still yearned for completeness. Frustrated on every count, Hayavadana is at last advised by the Bhagavata to try the Kali of mount chitrakoot, the goddess who is famous for being ever-awake to the call of devotees. Bhagavata sends Hayavadana to this temple along with the Actor blessing him thus "May you become successful in your search for completeness" (11).

There is a lot of comic irony in the way Hayavadana is transformed into a complete horse instead of turning into a complete man. On being asked by Bhagavata about the outcome of his prayers to the goddess, Hayavadana replies:

Ah! That's a long story, I went there, picked up a Sword.... Put it on my neck and said: 'Mother of all Nature, if you don't help me I'll chop off my head! (68)

Karnad never lost sight for the fact that he was writing for the modern theatregoers, for whom the contemporary idiom and ethos must be preserved. His treatment of myths leads to an absurdity of situation. In the recognition of this absurdity, lies the humour inherent in the situation. Hayavadana's account of the goddess's reaction has such comic-absurd implications:

Why don't you people go somewhere else if you want to chop off your stupid head? Why do you have to come to me?' I fell at her feet and said, 'Mother make me complete'. She said, 'So be it' and disappeared - even before I could say make me a complete man! I became a horse! (68)

This is how Hayavadana at last emerged as 'a full-fledged horse. Thus, his desire of becoming a complete man remains unfulfilled. The question remains unanswered as there has always been a dichotomy and opposition between the spiritual life and physical life. Whenever one tries to fathom deeper in search of completeness and perfection, one experiences a feeling of void within, of something missing that still remains to be discovered. The Vedas speak of the forefathers who have reached this goal, declaring that 'The priest of the world climb thee like a ladder, O hundred - peak to peak, there is made clear that much that has still to be done': (brahamanastva shatakrata ud kamsham iva yomire. Yat sanoh sanum aruhad bhuri aspasta kartvam) (Joshi, 23).

Similarly, Hayavadana's desire of becoming a complete man remains unfulfilled. His transformation to a horse is complete when his human voice ends up in a proper neigh from "Ha ! Ha ! Ha ! Ha !" to " HuhhuhHeahhh...." (70).

Hayavadana's myth seems to coalesce with the legend of Kapila and Devadatta by its emphasis on the importance of head vis-a-vis body. Just as the man with Devadatta's head is declared the husband of Padmini, similarly Hayavadana's head, which is that of a horse leads to his transformation into a horse. The body which is that of a man loses the claim to have a human head as well. The theme of incompleteness of ambiguity, and of doubleness is strengthened in the play by returning to the story of Devadatta and Kapila again. It is here that Karnad blends the main plot and the sub-plot of the play. The Bhagavata again turns thus: "Two friends there were-one mind, one heart. They saw a girl and forgot themselves. But they could not understand the song she sang". (11)

Devadatta is impatient to get Padmini as his wife, so much so that he would sacrifice his arms to the goddess Kali and his head to Lord Rudra. Kapila is assigned the task to find Padmini's house and convey Devadattaa's message. He goes to Pavana Veethi the street of merchants. After reaching there, he examines the doors one by one Karnad has intentionally added a myth again, this time of signs which are engraved on the doors of houses. Kapila says:

This is not a double-headed bird. It's an eagle - This Pavana - A lotus, this is- er-a lion. Tiger. A wheel. And this? God alone knows what this is. And the next? [In disgust] A horse! - a rhinoceros- another lion. Another lotus! (16)

It becomes obvious that the design on Padmini's door is that of a "two-headed bird," suggesting her future predicament. The lion and tiger symbol on the doors hints at Kapila and Devadatta the two protagonists of the play and 'A wheel' directly refers to the wheel of their fortune. 'A horse' is suggestive of Hayavadana in the main plot. Kapha on reaching Padmini's house, exclaims with wonder. "She's is Yakshini, Shakuntala, Urvashi, Indumati-all rolled into one" (16). Though pleading for Devadatta's marriage with Padmini, he himself develops infatuation for her.

Devadatta, my friend, I confess to you I'm feeling uneasy. You are a gentle soul.... She is not for the likes of you. What she needs is a man of steel.

However the things go in favour of Devadatta and Padmini is married to him. The old friendship of the two continues:

Devadatta Padmini - Kapila! To the admiring citizens of Dharampura, Rama-Sita Lakshmana. (16)

What begins with a simple love triangle ends in a comic and confusing twist of fate in Karnad's *Hayavadana.* Once Devadatta and Padmini embark on a journey with their friend Kapila. Devadatta, an insecure and jealous husband becomes suspicious of Padmini's love for Kapila and beheads himself in a temple of Goddess Kali. Kapila thinks he will be accused of having murdered the man for the sake of Padmini and beheads himself as well. Padmini, on finding the two dead, prepares to kill herself too, afraid of the scandal that is bound to follow. She is saved by Goddess Kali who comes to her rescue. Padmini then asks the goddess:

Can there ever be anything you already don't know, Mother? ..... Then why didn't you stop Devadatta when he came here? Why didn't you stop either of them? I would have been spared all this terror, this agony. Why did you wait so long? (32)

The goddess replies:

The rascals! They were lying to their last breaths. That fellow Devadatta - he had once promised his head to Rudra and his arms to me! Think of it - head to him and arms to me! Then because you insisted on going to the Rudra temple, he comes here and offers his head. Nobly too - wants to keep his word, he says - no other reason! ...Then this Kapila: ....! Says he is dying for friendship. (33)

The goddess's reaction reminds us of the Hindu belief that if you promise something to offer to God and if your wish comes true then you should do it whole heartedly or else God's wrath will fall upon you. Karnad incorporates the Hindu ritual of praying to goddess Kali for wish fulfilment as means of satirizing Hindu religious practices. It is a widespread notion in India that people turn to gods only when they want something. If their desires are not fulfilled they deny the presence of gods. This mindset and superstitious beliefs are mocked at by Karnad. Goddess Kali appears before Padmini, who speaks the truth and for the 'liars' that is Kapila and Devadatta she had only anger. After Padmini pleads before goddess Kali and when the goddess asks her to put the heads of two on their bodies, Padmini interchanges their heads. Devadatta and Kapila stare at each other:

DEVADATTA: Mixed-up heads!

KAPILA: Heads mixed up!

DEVADATTA; Exchanged heads!

KAPILA: Heads Exchanged!

And the three sing together:

What a good mix!

No more tricks!

Is this one that or that one this?

Ho! Ho! (35)

Erin B. Mee notes that through "Karnad refuses to define the theatre of roots movement, he does say 'it does not reject music like the western realistic theatre'..." (Mee, 147). Mee also points out that Karnad credits B.V. Karanth's production "with bringing music back to the Indian stage" (Mee, 147). The songs in *Hayavadana*, therefore, have immense significance. They add to the sense of performance in the play. The play acquires great intensity as songs of the characters and the chorus create an intensity, which is augmented by inviting a direct involvement of the audience, as Bhagvata asks questions in the manner of Vetal.

When the friends are brought back to life, both of them claim to be husbands of Padmini. Devadatta's point is that "According to the Shastras, the head is the sign of the man..."(38). Kapila claims that he has the body she has lived with all these months and the child she is carrying is the seed of his body. The body-intellect divide, and the controversy, of this perplexing situation is very significantly dramatized by Karnad. The doubleness of the situation becomes more concrete when Kapila says to Padmini.

I know what you want. Padmini, Devadatta's clever head and Kapha's strong body.... (38)

The problem becomes more complex and persists till a solution is found to it. The question is that who is now the real husband, the one with the husband's head or the one with his body? Act one ends with the Bhagavata posing a question to the audience in the manner of Vetala of

Vetalapanchvimshika as to who is the rightful husband of Padmini. Act two opens with the Bhagavata thinking of a solution which holds the entire future of "the three unfortunate beings." (40) The Chorus sings in this context:

The future pointed out by the tongue safe inside the skull is not acceptable to us. We must read the forehead which Brahma has disconnected from the entrails. We must unravel the net on the palm disclaimed by the brain. We must plumb the hidden depths of the rivers running under our veins... (40)

Karnad uses Bhagavata as his spokesperson who highlights certain aspects of the play which help us in understanding the play better. The ongoing complexity in the play is well analysed by the Bhagavata. He offers a solution and his rational and logical answer is supported by the sacred texts which appeal to the audience. The three friends go to a great rishi, who perhaps remembering what King Vikrama had said, gave the solution.

As the heavenly Kalpa Vriksha is supreme among trees, as is the head among human limbs. Therefore, the man with Devadatta's head is indeed Devadatta and he is the rightful husband of Padmini. (40)

The answer given in the *Kathasaritsagar* is: since the head represents the man, the person with the husband's head is the real husband. If the head is the determining limit, then the body should change to fit the head. The same happens in the play. The question of identity is, thus, solved. With the passage of time, things change and the bodies and the mind accept each other and become a whole.

Karnad brings in two living dolls at this juncture. These dolls lay bare the inner psyche of Padmini by referring to her dream about Kapila, whose body she desires but being a married woman, cannot express herself. The dolls also indulge in gossip and bring in an element of humour too:

DOLL I: He goes to her.

DOLL II: ... very near her...

DOLL I: What's he going to do now?

DOLL II: What?

DOLL I: But he's climbing tree!

DOLL II: He's dived into a river!

DOLL I: Is that all he came for? (50)

Referring directly to Padmini's dream, they remind one of the gossiping neighbours:

DOLL II: It was so shameless...

DOLL II: I said be quiet...

DOLL II: Honestly! The way they ... (51)

They notice the slow process of change in Devadatta's body and also comment on certain very important aspects of the play which add to its thematic development:

DOLL I: His palms! They are so rough....Like a labourer's but now they are soft -sickly soft life a young girl's.

DOLL II: I know I've noticed something too.

DOLL I: What?

DOLL I: His stomach. It was so tight and muscular. Now...

DOLL I: I know: It's loose.... (47)

This pair of dolls acquires more importance when Padmini sends Devadatta to the Ujjain fair to purchase new dolls. These dolls were bought by Devadatta before the birth his child, they were worn out, and therefore, were to be replaced. Erin B. Mee points out:

The Dolls allow Karnad to introduce the voice of 'society' into what is otherwise a three-character story. The dolls are not at all 'necessary' to the plot, which could move forward without them, but they are important because they remind spectators of the presence of society—and of propriety. Their attitudes contribute to the motivating force for Padmini's behaviour; some of what she does is because *of what society will say, and some of her actions are* in spite of *what society will say. (146)*

A large funeral pyre is made and Padmini performs 'Sati' with the bodies of Devadatta and Kapila. There is tragic irony in the way Padmini articulates her pain as she performs 'Sati'. She expresses her grief and helplessness to Goddess Kali.

Fig. IV: Padmini praying to goddess Kali.

Source: Sangeet Natak Akademi, New Delhi.

Kali Mother of all Nature, you must have your joke even now, other women can die praying that they should get the same husband in all the lives to come. You haven't left me even that little consolation. (63)

The note of defiance is associated with Padmini throughout the play. She defies convention in not holding on to one man all her life. Her myth epitomizes the deflation of the'Sati' myth itself. This idea is reinforced further when the female chorus sings referring to the tree of Fortunate lady.

Why should love stick to the sap of a single body?... Why should it be tied down to the relation of a single flower?... A head for each arm. I have neither regret nor shame. The blood pours into the earth and a song branches out in the sky. (63-64)

Through chorus, Karnad invites his audiences to re-interpret the myths. The song questions the very concept of the cherished ideal of Indian womanhood. It is a celebration of freedom. Padmini voices unequivocally that she is neither ashamed nor regretful about the choice she made in her life. Karnad's handling of the mythic legend is revolutionary in this respect. Bhagvata's prayer in the end is given an ironic twist. As he prays for good rains, good crops, prosperity in science, poetry et al, he concludes by saying:

Give the rulers of our country success in all endeavours and along with it, a little bit of sense. (71)

The chorus performs a very significant role in the play. It is the voice of the spirit of modernity. The audiences are asked by the chorus not to:

... judge Padmini according to orthodox social conventions as expressed by the Dolls, or at the very least to recognize these social strictures as conventions rather than inherent truths . Karnad wants his audience to examine these conventional attitudes and think about whom they serve. Thus, every theatrical device Karnad introduces offers another way of understanding Padmini, and another perspective on her situation. (Mee, 147)

Karnad begins the play with Nandi (singing of benedictory verse) and concludes it with the Bharatavakya (valedictory prayer), recalling the tradition of ancient Sanskrit drama. But the ritualistic invocation of Lord Ganesha, the elephant-headed God, in the Nandi and the Bharatavakya goes beyond the fulfilment of a traditional prescription and assumes symbolic significance.

As the embodiment of imperfection, the play revolves around the image of Lord Ganesha, which operates at several levels. The new image suggests a major development in the action as well as the central theme of completeness of being. The motif of transposed heads is further extended to the story Kapila and Devadatta. The multilayered structure of the play points towards a single meaning, that is, the eternal search for perfection and completeness.

Karnad ventures into the realm of traditional theatre, deeply rooted in religious sensibility so as to make 'the paraphernalia of folk theatre meaningful and relevant in the modern context'. The play *Hayavadana* chooses for its narrative the ambience of folk drama, and incorporates the elements of *Yakshagana* (a folk theatre form of Karnataka).

Hayavadana brings together elements of modern urban theatre with elements of *Yakshagana* to create a new genre of Indian theatre. The play challenges the "colonial culture by confronting its aesthetic assumptions and the structures it privileges; but by resisting false cultural and national essentialisms" (Mee, 173). It is a perfect example of hybrid theatre which came to "represent the new dramaturgy and playwriting practices of the theatre of roots" (Mee-174).

In the backdrop of classical Sanskrit drama, Karnad "employs the conventions of folk tales and motifs of folk theatre i.e. masks, curtains, mime, songs, the commentator-narrator, dolls, house-man, the story within-a-story and presents an amalgam of the human and the non-human, to create a strange magical world" (Goel, 204). The element of the supernatural also plays a significant role in the play. All these folk theatre strategies are used by Karnad with great dexterity as thematic and technical devices.

The two plots which constitute the fabric of *Hayavadana*, the main plot (in the . transposition of heads) and the sub-plot (in the story of Hayavadana) depict that 'perfection is a humanly unfeasible idea'. A complex pattern of relationships is built up by the multiplicity of the characters and their individual psychic circles playing into each other. 'The mythical figure of lord Ganesha who is the central whole of the play represents a perfect blend of three different worlds of experience,— the divine, the human and the animal.

This is where the three mythic legends converge. Karnad's handling of the motif of the transposed head is, thus, immaculate. The three myths narrate different stories yet are based on a single idea pertaining to the quest for completeness and perfection, which is hard to fulfil. As these stories are retold, they drive home the point, the playwright intends to make. *Hayavadana* is a masterpiece where myths bring into prominence the thematic implications of the play better than any of the mode of expression.

Naga-Mandala: Transforming Fantasy into Theatre

Naga-Mandala is another award-winning play of Girish Karnad, which won him the Karnataka Sahitya Academy Award for the most creative work of 1989.The play was produced for the first time in the year 1988.Staged at the

Rock Garden, Chandigarh, for ten successive days, it became immensely popular in the North India as well.

Indian folk traditions are among the oldest and the richest in the world. The folklorists classify traditional stories as myths, legends and folktales. They define folktales as the stories which include fairies, witches and animal characters. A folktale invariably carries some of its cultural contents within it; it is also a travelling metaphor that acquires a new meaning and dimension with every re-telling. A branch of science that deals with the study of folk tales with its prime focus on the 'archetypical quality of truth', (Wikipedia, 7) is known as folkloristics. A.K. Ramanujan, a great critic-scholar has made significant contribution to the field of Indian and South Asian folklore. He once remarked that Indian thinking is "context sensitive". In his work in folklore studies, Ramanujan highlights the intertextuality of the Indian oral and written literary tradition (Bande, The Tribune, 5).

In *Naga-Mandala*, Karnad takes recourse to folk tales and myths associated with them. Karnad turns away from the 'classical' tradition as his source to local Kannada folk-tales in *Nagamandala*. The play is based upon two oral tales from Karnataka which Karnad had heard from Professor A.K. Ramanujan, who had collected many folk tales and their variants as they existed in different parts of India. Here he combines two tales, the central one focuses on the snake-lover motif, while the frame story explores the notion of stories having a life "independent of their narrators, derived from oral traditions" (Chatterji, 3).

The title of the play comes not from any human character, but from a snake the Naga, that is the Cobra. The reference to the Cobra in the title suggests that Karnad not merely tries to dramatize and interpret the folk tales in the modern context but also suggests deeper and hidden meanings at various levels.

In *Naga-Mandala* Karnad draws heavily on the myth of the supposed powers of the Naga to transform itself into any shape. The significance of the play, however, extends much beyond the surface charm and simplicity of the tale of a serpent. What is foregrounded is the essential reality associated with the "experience of man and woman in the psychological transitory phase" (Gupta, 250) of growth into selfhood. The serpent myth is also used to highlight the essentially feministic bias of the play.

Karnad has subtitled the play as 'Play with a Cobra', which directly hints at the theme and significance of the role of the cobra in the play. Naga is the snake god, who grants the wish for fertility. Mandala is a tantric concept which indicates inner concentration, a source of energy. Thus, *Naga-Mandala* incorporates magico-ritualistic principles. As already noted, Karnad weaves into the play two Kannada folk tales which belong to the oral traditions of literarure in India and have an existence of their own, surviving only as they are passed on from one story-teller to another. The play has also been hailed as an example of hybrid theatre. Like *Hayavadana*, JVaga-Mandala also combines the traditions of folk theatre and western dramaturgy.

The play tells the story of Rani, newly married to Appanna, and their 'gradual understanding of the role, function and responsibilities of the institution of marriage' (Gupta,250). The play is a powerful portrait of the agony and perplexity faced by men and women as they step into adulthood. Karnad is particularly interested in highlighting the suffering of Rani as she hovers between conflicting predicaments of being rejected and wooed at the same time.

Naga-Mandala begins with a 'Prologue' which takes the audience into the inner sanctum of a ruined temple. The presiding deity of the temple cannot be identified as the idol is broken. A man, sitting there in a morose stance, tells the audience that he must stay awake the whole night because he has the curse of death on him. His fault is that he has written "plays...staged them [and] caused so many good people ...to fall asleep twisted in miserable chairs..." (1-2). A mendicant had advised him that if he could keep awake at least one whole night, he would not die. The day is the last day of the month, and he has to keep himself awake in order to overcome the curse of death. He then swears to himself that if he could survive that night without sleep, he would have nothing more to do with story writing, he will "abjure all story- telling, all play-acting"(2).

The play opens with a note of comic irony in the presence of a doubtful deity, which makes assertion of the speakesr sound even more doubtful. The situation is absurd and deeply ironic. The Neitzchian stance cannot be overlooked too. The absent god reminds one of the dead god as well:

So I have fled from home and come to this temple, nameless and empty. (2)

Then suddenly the audience is transported to a fantasy-filled atmosphere with the entry of four lamp flames who talk to each other in female voices. This bewilders the man as well as the audiences. Karnad's presentation of such a spectacle is aimed at arresting the sensibility of the spectators. The man in the play directly expresses his astonishment:

MAN: I don't believe it! They are naked lamp flames ! No wicks, No lamps. No one holding them. Just lamp flames on their own... floating in the air ! Is that even possible?(2)

As the ritualistic aura grips the atmosphere, more magic is woven into the fabric of the play. Karnad says that the writer had heard that in some remote villages, the flames had the ability to speak and could talk to each other with female voices. All these flames are not mere flames, they serve to tear asunder the hypocrisy of society, showing forth the moral debasement of people. They play, therefore, is a reflection on the decadent values of a sick society.

Flame 1 says that her master was a miser and hence had put the lights off early and due to this she could come to the temple early. Flame 2 says that she came from a family, whose master was a 'lustful man'. He needed the light to feast on his wife's body. Flame 3 says that, hereafter she could come early because her master and wife were free now to enjoy worldly pleasures. The master's mother had died and now both of them were free to enjoy.

Flame 4 has a different story to tell. The lady in her house suspected her husband and she had a story and a song inside her mouth, which she kept to herself. She did not reveal it to anybody. One day, while she was snoring, the story and the song jumped out of her mouth. The story became a lady and the song took the form of a saree. When the woman woke up, she saw a young lady, coming out of her husband's room. Thus, these turn out to be some hallucinations in the mind of the woman. The story and the song then begin to tell a new story.

Karnad's flames are women—women as story tellers. This image is crystallized further with the reference made by the flame to the old woman, who once again emerges as a story teller. The play thus, focuses on the creative impulses of women. The tale of the old woman, who lived with the song and the story, that finally found freedom of expression is narrated thus:

This afternoon... the story and the song jumped out... [and] the story took the form of a young woman and the song became a sari. The young woman wrapped herself in the sari and stepped out... (40)

The identification of the flames with young and sprightly local women, and the stories that they tell each other is a brilliant device used by Karnad for creating a particularly female context and content in the 'male-oriented folk tale'. He builds up within the play a relationship that exists between oral narrative tradition and female experiences as expressed in female narratives.

Karnad says that women tell stories when putting children to bed or while doing their household chores. Old women in the family usually narrate the folktales, either when the children are being fed in the evenings or when they are put to bed in the night. Though they are narrated to children, stories serve as a parallel system of communication among women in the family. 'In the presence of other women and children, women give expression to their own points of view and experiences which are not perhaps permitted or recognized by patriarchal, classical stories' (Gupta, 251). In the course of telling these tales, they mix the folk tales, myths and legends and while narrating they often mould, add, reinvent and transform them. After introducing an unambiguous note of feminine sensibility, in the 'prologue', the main plot of *Naga-Mandala* begins to unfold:

A young girl. Her name... it doesn't matter. But she was an only daughter. So her parents called her Rani, Queen...Queen of long tresses. For when her hair was tied up in a knot, it was as though a black king cobra lay curled on the nape of her neck... (6)

The very beginning of the play introduces us to the central characters of the play, Rani is referred to as a Queen. Ironically she lives like a slave and the king cobra lives very near to her in her tresses. The story deals with the life of Rani and Appanna. They are not given any name in the beginning and hence they represent the whole humankind. Rani is so called because she is the queen of the long tresses, which, when tied into a knot, resembles a 'cobra'. Rani is married to Appanna which means 'any man'. The story states that the main characters' names are not important and adds that 'any common name would do'. In this sense Karnad appears to be universalizing the characters. They are every man and woman, as the experiences that they undergo have universal significance.

Appanna and Rani are married. Rani apparently, being a child bride is bought to her husband's house after gaining puberty. Appanna is not a faithful husband and treats her with contempt, aggression and mistrust. He spends his time with his concubine and comes to his house only to have his lunch. He speaks to Rani only in monosyllables. Their marriage is a failure, which results in Rani's isolation and forces her to create a fantasy world of her own. She imagines herself to be a princess locked up by a demon.

RANI: So the demon locks her up in his castle. Then it rains for seven days and seven nights.... Then, a big whale comes to Rani and says, 'Come, Rani, let us go. (14)

Here Karnad lends a western flavour to the play by referring to a classical western fairy tale situation, where a demon imprisons a princess. Rani leads a secluded life and then Kurudawa saves her. It is only she who understands Rani's real problem. Kurudavva gives two small roots to Rani and asks her to mix it in Appanna's food. It is believed that, by taking the root, Appanna will not go and visit the concubine again. Kurudawa says, "Once he gets even the smell of yours he won't go after that concubine". The first root has no effect on Appanna. Rani takes a bigger root, and when she mixes it in the curry it becomes bloody red. She actually curses herself for trying to give this to Appanna. Rani envisions,

"Suppose it harms my husband, what will happen to me?" She spills it on a nearby anthill. A snake living in the anthill instantly falls in love with Rani.

The snake is believed to be a symbol of fertility. The snake takes the shape of Appanna and has sexual communion with Rani. It is through the snake that Rani understands the meaning and passion of love in marital life. Her unfulfilled desires of married life are gratified by the snake lover. To feed Rani's sexual, physical and emotional needs, the Naga provides her with love in the guise of Appanna .He visits her at nights and Rani surrenders her soul and body to his love and affection. She becomes pregnant and when the real Appanna gets to know about it, he calls her a "whore." and charges her with adultery. Rani is put to trial by Appanna in front of village elders. Rani is asked by the village leaders to perform the ordeal of holding hot iron rod to demonstrate that she is a chaste woman and faithful to her hushand. The snake advises her to perform the ordeal of holding the snake instead. Rani proves her chastity and declares:

I have held by this hand, only two... Yes, my husband, and this king Cobra. Except for these two, I have not touched any of the male sex. (39)

She further adds that if she is lying "let the cobra bite her". The Cobra doesn't bite her, instead it spreads its hood on her head and sways it gently and hangs like a garland around her neck and then slips back into the ant-hill. The elders on the village judicial committee proclaim her to be a 'goddess.' The elders tell Appanna that his wife is a goddess incarnate and the couple, being seated in the palanquin, is taken in a procession to their house. Appanna begs her forgiveness and spends the rest of his life in her service.

Karnad himself refers to the oral tales as particularly responsive to feminine sensibility. The world of these tales is a world where women understand the pain of women. Thus, the myth of root in the plot is very significant. Like most folktales, supernatural elements play a vital role in *Nagamandala*. Traditional beliefs help generate supernatural elements. There is always some magical power in specific roots as per traditional beliefs. Kurudawa the blind woman is more sensitive towards the agony of Rani than anyone else. She gives her the magical root to cook curry with, and give it to Appanna. Rani, however, is terrified on seeing that the curry looked like blood and throws it into the ant-hill, where the snake lived, instead of giving it to Appanna. The root is consumed by a king cobra which results in very interesting twists and turns in the play. It is the Cobra, therefore, on whom the potion has the desired effect. He is irresistibly drawn towards Rani. Ultimately, however, Rani gets everything she desired.

Another belief is that the cobra has the divine power and it can assume any form. In the play, Naga takes the form of Appanna. It is out of union with the form of Appanna that Rani gets pregnant. So, in some sense, Rani has nothing to do with this "unlawful" sexual communion. It is with his supernatural powers that Naga saves Rani from her pitiable and dangerous plight to prove her chastity.

The myths of giving men potions to win them over are age old. They are mostly part of folk stories which are, sometimes purely products of wishful thinking. Karnad has handled this mythic aspect of folk imagination with a rare sensitivity. The story of Appanna also has certain interesting touches. It is believed that some witch or fairy enchanted him away from his lawful wife. In folk lore the act of the unfaithful husband is often explained away by referring to some mysterious fairy. The identity of the woman who entices Appanna away is unknown and it remains a mystery. These anecdotal explanations generally intended to justify that human beings are simply pawns in the hands of the divine or supernatural powers.

Makrand Paranjape in his essay refers to an academic paper in the shape of a play being presented by the sutradhar. The play is in the 'manner of Girish Karnad', 'a play redolent with myth and mystery, with masks and music, in a word, a play as a ritual' (Paranjape, 63). He refers to shape-shifting as a central metaphor in Girish Karnad's plays which is used as structural and thematic device. In cultural anthropology and folklore shape-shifting is a term used to describe the transformations that are common in the myths and folklore of most cultures. For example when a plant turns into an animal or when a woman gets transformed into a bird or when a person becomes someone else by changing shape or adopts any other form in any way.

Numerous examples of shape shifting are found in Indian epics, Puranas and folk tales. Karnad draws heavily upon such resources in most of his plays. In *Nagamandala* the shape shifting is discernible in the transformation of the Naga into the snake lover. The technique of shape shifting has been effectively used by Karnad, "as a means of reviving the ancient and sacred function of drama as ritual" (Josipura, 261). The cobra assumes the forms of Appanna to make love to Rani, the flames transforms into human characters to gossip at the temple. The story told by the old woman changes into a song and a sari. In the discourse on shape-shifting Makrand Paranjape elaborately explains its meaning and importance. He states:

... shape-shifting is a universal motif which does not however, have a uniform significance ... its meanings and functions change depending on the context.

[For him]...shape-shifting is a way of exploring similarity and difference... it proves the underlying unity in the substratum of life while allowing multitudinous diversity on the surface. (95)

The emphasis is on the idea that we are all made up of the same building blocks, all life is similar and can be transformed from one form to the other. Applying this definition to literature he adds:

... literature and myth merely dramatize, heighten and highlight what is theoretically possible in nature and science. (89)

Pranjape relates shape-shifting to Karnad's practice of playwrighting. He is of the view that

... it is like an equation or a theorem. Something is posited through a hypothesis, and then worked out in the body of the play. Shape-shifting at least in Karnad's plays is a means to work out some ideas... the playwright forces us to think by

introducing such thought situations through the artifice of shape-shifting. (89)

Shape-shifting is very deeply imbued in the spirit of drama itself. An actor playing a character pretends to be someone else in a play and therefore the whole notion of drama depends on shape-shifting. A mask, which is the central metaphor of theatre, is also symbolic of shape-shifting.

... shape-shifting in Karnad is ... a central structural strategy [and works as] a means of retaining the ancient and sacred function of drama as ritual. (90)

Referring to the 'preconditions and consequences', of shape-shifting which is prevalent in folklore and myth, Paranjape states "shape-shifting is to be found in non-realistic fantasies, fables, myths, or folk tales. It is associated with the supernatural, and requires special powers and might have unpleasant consequences" (Paranjape,90). In Karnad's plays the outcome of shape-shifting can be seen in the form of 'disastrous consequences'. The play might have unhappy ending, there might be chaos, destruction and tragic death of the protagonist in the end.

It is often seen in his plays that he who transgresses must pay the price like Naga in *Nagamandala* who must die when his shape-shifting is found out. Another precondition for shape-shifting is that it takes place under unusual circumstances under some spell or at the behest of a powerful person. In *Hayavadana*, Padmini seeks a boon from the goddess so that the heads can be transposed. In *Tughlaq*, Muhammad's attempt to change the capital to Daulatabad is because of the power he assumes. In *Nagamandala* the shape-shifting occurs after the old woman's potion affects the Naga. In these three plays the outcome of shape-shifting is tragic.

The ending of the play has something more for the audience. The Man and the Story offer an alternate ending and discuss the inappropriateness of the present ending. The Man seems to be the metaphor for the playwright and his critical faculty, the Story is his poetic imagination and the Flames may stand for both the village women and the audience (Jalote, Epic Theatre, 272).

The folkloric element once again takes precedence over everything else. In folklore, one story leads to another. Besides, there is freedom to choose endings. The Man argues that the present ending just doesn't work and feels pity for Appanna as he will spend the rest of his days in misery. In a soliloquy Appanna reveals :

What am I to do? Is the whole world against me ?...I know I haven't slept with my wife. Let the world say what it likes. Let any miracle declare her a goddess. But I know ! What sense am I to make of my life if that's worth nothing?(41)

The Story expresses her views and questions Rani's acceptance of Appanna's form as her real husband:

No two men make love alike. And that night...When her true husband climbed into bed with her, How could she fail to realize it was someone new? (41)

The story insists that Rani knew the reality or else she would have cried out in anguish when 'this conundrum had spread his hood out at her' (41). The Man suggests that the ending lacks reference to the Cobra and is not complete. He then formulates a new story:

One day the Cobra was sitting in his Ant-hill and it thought of Rani and said: 'Why should I not go and take a look?(42)

The Cobra once again transforms itself into a Naga and enters Rani's house where she is sleeping with her child and husband. The Naga cannot bear to see Rani in another man's arm. Infuriated, he decides that someone has to die. He cannot kill Rani because he loves her passionately. He summons his magical powers and becomes the size of her tresses. And ties a knot into a noose and places it around her neck. When Rani wakes up, her head weighs a ton, there is something caught up in tresses Appanna combs her hair and a dead cobra falls on the ground.

Astonished by the sight Appanna says 'you are no common person'. Her long hair saved them all. And once again she is considered as a goddess. Now Rani insists that the Cobra be virtually cremated and the pyre should be lit by their son. She also wishes that every year their son should perform the ritual to commemorate its death.

Karnad has presented us with two different endings and has used the legends in a very fascinating manner where one has the flexibility to change the ending according to one's desire. As mentioned earlier, the play is based on oral tales which permit the narrator to mix, mould, reinvent and transform the tale so as to present an absorbing and engaging story as per his own or the wishes of the audience.

The flames present their views and remark that it has become a tragic story with an unhappy ending, but the man makes a significant remark, that death is an inescapable truth. Ironically he himself wants to escape his death as the mendicant has told him to stay awake all night or else he'll die. So he continues and again formulates the story, this time with a happy ending. Rani and Appanna are sleeping with their child. Suddenly Rani gets up holding her hair, says that her head is paining. Appanna combs her hair and a live snake falls out of her hair and lies writhing on the floor. Appanna runs out to search for a stick to kill the snake. Rani, knowing that it is Naga lets her hair down to the floor and hides the snake in her tresses. She talks to the Cobra softly:

RANI : What are you doing here ? He'll kill you. Go. Go away....Why did you ever come in here, stupid?... My hair Of course. Come quick. Climb into it... Are you safely in there? Good. Now stay there. (45)

She tells the Naga that her hair is the symbol of her wedded bliss, asking it to live in there, for ever. The Flames disappear one by one. We are brought back to the inner sanctum of the temple. The man is sitting there alone. It is morning, he bows to the audience and goes out.

The tale unravels the complexity of human relationships. Karnad uses the folktale in the Indian context to reveal the prejudices and dilemmas within the matrix of social and individual relations. Karnad has presented a metaphysical world where things happen inexplicably and the intentions of people do not govern their actions (Joshipura, 26). Man-woman intimate relationships, the question of chastity being imposed on married women while their husbands have a merry-go-round with other women outside their wedlock, married women's earnest desire for the love of their husbands in spite of the shortcomings of their husbands are themes that directly attack the male dominated society. Rani's predicament poignantly reflects the human need to live by fictions and half truths. She sees her husband in two unconnected roles - as a stranger during the day and as a lover at night (Joshipura, 262). Her suffering after marriage and her oppression by Appanna give the play a feminist stance. The play questions the patriarchal moral code which demands the faithfulness of a woman to her husband but not of a man to his wife. She is also suppressed by the Naga who asks her not to question anything which leads to her failure to discover the truth about him.

The secret love that Naga demonstrates by his killing himself on the passionate and warm body of Rani, and, above all, the result of the sexual communion being a male child, the "son" lighting funeral pyre and so many other potent and hidden meanings, make this play a very complex play. Dolly George comments:

The village judicial system also comes to be portrayed with ease, and with this the process of deification in Indian society also gets revealed. Demonstration of unusual power and tolerance is sure ground and an essential step toward deification. (George, 4)

The mythical significance of the play can also be seen in the reference to the Mandala. A Mandala is a geometric figure based upon the squaring of a circle around a unifying centre. It stands for the desire for spiritual unity and psychic integration. "In its classic Asian form, the Mandala juxtaposes the triangle, the square, and the circle with their numerical equivalents of three, four, and seven. The circle represents wholeness, as desired by Rani in the play, number three represents the male principle, spiritual awareness and unity. No. 4 is associated with the female principles, and the four elements (earth, air, fire, water) and number seven is the most potent of all symbolic numbers -signifying the union of three and four, the completion of a cycle, a perfect order. The male and the female principles are unified in number seven which constitutes the circle of the classical form of Mandala."(Gurine, 161).

As pointed out earlier, in one of the alternative endings provided in the play, Rani also insists that the Naga be cremated with sanctity and the rituals of his death be commemorated every year. The idea of worshipping the Naga is introduced once again. The serpent, particularly in the Western thought is associated with evil and energy too, which must be tamed with love. Though there is hardly any reference to Naga's evil powers in the play, yet in one of the alternate endings he does feel the pangs of jealousy. But Rani's love seems to tame his negative energy and he lets himself be killed.

The idea of suggesting alternative endings bring in the elements of the Brechtian theatre, whereby audience participation becomes important. The narrator and the flames directly address the audience, inviting their participation. Thus, emotional involvement of the audience is minimized and they are provoked to think. *Naga-Mandala* thus combines the western and the oriental dramaturgies, much in the manner of hybrid theatre.

Flowers: Saga of Body and Soul

Flowers is based on a folk-tale from Chitradurga region in Karnataka. Karnad returns to the world of folklore and takes up the legend Veerana, which became popular when the Kannada writer T.R. Subbanna included it in his novel, *Hamsageethe* (Swan Song). Karnad's monologue is a swan song of a different kind. It highlights "the spiritual and aesthetic intensity with which the priest has devoted himself to the task of worshipping and beautifying the iingam' - an intensity that is transferred to the body of the courtesan - mistress" (xxxii).

Karnad reinvents the folktale that deals with a Brahmin priest who is lost in his spiritual adoration of Shiva and the sexual intimacy with the courtesan Chandravate, M.K. Rukhaya comments:

By juxtaposing two complementary entities pertaining to "sophisticated" culture, the playwright appears to say-- If the first is divine and the second beautiful; cannot the divine be beautiful and the beautiful divine? (1)

Karnad's play revolves around a priest who has lived all his life is isolation and 'discouraged all friendly attentions from the world outside' (Karnad,Vol.2,243). The priest has a routine of visiting the temple daily and decorating the Shiva linga in a different way every day. It has become a part of his daily ritual and a sacred act. He is in a way obsessed with the lingam which for him is so real that he talks and sings to it and even discusses political issues with it. His wife calls the lingam his 'step-wife'. The priest remarks that "a conversation (is) conducted through flowers - malligai, sevanti, chendu hoovu, sampigai and Kanankambara" (244). It was during the Shivaratri celebrations that Ranganayaki a courtesan comes into his life. The courtesan visits the temple during the festival and the priest is attracted towards her.

I mechanically took the coconut she offered, broke it, placed the prasada inside the turned to hand it back. She was bending, holding the pallu of her sari spread out in front of her. The upper half of her bosom was uncovered..., I saw the mole. On her left breast, just near the cleavage. I looked up at her. There must have been something unusual in my movement, for she looked up too and caught my eyes. (245)

Her visits become a routine and the priest waits for a glimpse of her. The priest remarks T wanted her. I had never lusted for a woman before and so felt emasculated by this sudden weakness. Yet I could not control the fire raging in my loins" (245). Everyday he waits upon to see her and offer her the Prasad. One day she fails to come at the temple and the priest visits her house to inquire about her. Ranganayaki tells him that it is because of her menstrual seclusion that she didn't come to the temple. She requests him to come again after she has had her cleansing bath. Ranganayaki wants the priest to embellish her body with flowers, the way he decorates the lingam. As he would decorate the courtesan the linga poses a question to him 'Why didn't the Lord offer a form which inflamed invention like Ranga did?'(250) Decking her up becomes the daily routine, 'never exactly the repeatable'.

One day, the chieftain of the region visits the temple late at midnight. His unexpected arrival makes the priest little nervous, as the priest is at that time at Ranganayaki's house decorating her with flowers. As soon as he hears the canon sound, he rushes to the temple and starts decorating the lingam with the same flowers, which he had used on Ranganayaki's body. He himself calls them 'the leavings, polluted discards'. The flowers are faded but the pooja is performed. As the priest holds out the plate of flowers so that the chieftan could pick his choice of flower as prasada. The chieftan notices a long hair in the flowers and questions the priest. 'I didn't know God had long hair' (256). A chill invades the sanctum and the priest gives the only reply possible under the circumstances. 'If we believe that God has long hair, He will have long hair' (257).

The question is- highly suggestive as Lord Shiva (obviously) does wear his hair long. So the connotation here is to definitely ascertain God's identity in terms of gender. Cannot God be a woman? Moreover, the term 'linga' also refers to the grammatical concept of gender ... without any prefix is neutral here. This is precisely the implication here that God is beyond the concept of gender. (Rukhaya, 1)

The unflinching faith of the priest is put to test and after a week's rigorous penance he succeeds in proving his spiritual bondage with the linga. After twelve days when he opened the door of the sanctum there was a huge crowd and the chieftain waiting to pass the judgement. As the sanctum is lit by sunlight, one could see long cascading hair on the linga, "waves and waves of jet black hair came billowing out, their tips gently eddying and swirling in the evening breeze" (258). One of the Brahmin courtiers tugs a tuft of hair and it bleeds at the root, he cries hysterically, 'It's bleeding. It's bleeding. I have wounded God' (259). The priest is taken home by his wife where he falls into deep sleep and wakes up refreshed. His wife informs him that Ranganayaki has left the town. The courtesan is gone and has been replaced by Lord Shiva.

By the end of the monologue the priest is transformed into a new state of spiritual adulthood. Karnad here reminds us of the hero archetypes who undertake some arduous journey and perform impossible tasks. He passes from ignorance to social and spiritual awakening. The priest tries to seek answers to some of the puzzling questions put forward by God. He contemplates:

Why has God done this to me? I had only asked Him to give me the courage to live in disgrace, for I knew I had tainted myself... I am guilty of gross dereliction, of sacrilege. Guilty of cruelty to the two women I loved. Why then should God cast His vote on my behalf? Because I loved Him? Has God the right to mock justice in favour of love for Him? Or does He have a different logic? (260)

The Scorpio constellation, with which Karnad begins his monologue, crawls and its reflection floats in the hollow water. The priest expresses his desire to seek the answers that

God has denied him, in the narrow confines of that hollow. Karnad uses the water image to strengthen the point that the identity of the priest transforms, undergoes a change and he wishes to dissolve in water "the identities of religious adoration and sexual devotion, marginalizing social boundaries and conventions" (Rukhaya, 2). The body and soul conflict is well portrayed by Karnad and he uses it as the underlying theme to exhibit the priest's internal conflict between devotion to God and love. Aparna Dharwadker aptly remarks:

The mingling of the spiritual and the carnal is short-lived, however. The miracle of the shivalinga confirms the power of the priest's worship and marks him as one of the chosen, but it also ends his life, (xxxii)

Dharwadker also points out that "The introspective, confessional male voice of the priest in *Flowers* has no precursor in Karnad's drama" (xxxii). She suggests a close parallel between Karnad's priest and Praneshacharya in U.R.Anantha Murthy's *Samskara* as "...both men sublimate their sexuality into religious fervour, and find sudden release after a lifetime of repression in an illicit union....Furthermore both versions offer an ironic variation on what the West calls the whore-Madonna syndrome...." (Aparna Dharwadker, Vol.2,xxxii-xxxiii).The monologue associates the thrill and sensuality with courtesan and dullness and routine with priest's wife. To quote Dharwadker again:

This is arguably a chauvinistic position, though in Karnad's portrayal the priest's voice has an endearing innocence and honesty rather than an alienating arrogance, (xxxiii)

The monologue addresses a complex problem in the modern context while treating a folk tale as a central metaphor. The basic idea is actually associated with the limits of human condition vis-a-vis the line of demarcation between one kind of devotion and the other kind of devotion and the innate tendency of man to dissolve the dividing line between the two in order to sublimate the experience and attain salvation. What makes this short monologue significant is the theme of eternal conflict between repression and indulgence and between austerity and passion. These are issues of timeless relevance and continue to puzzle writers interminably.

Chapter-4
Resurrecting History as Contemporaneity

In the roots movement is inherent the 'Idea of India', a phrase used by Sunil Khilnani, where he talks about the nationalist idea of a unified India also propagated by Nehru and Gandhi. In the modern context India can be seen as a nation known by its multiculturalism and multi-religious practices. Nehru referred to the concept of 'unity in diversity' so as to define a nation ". . . [which] discovered a basis for unity both in a shared historical past of cultural mixing, and a future project of common development"(Khilnani,154). It was this thought of uniting democracy, religious tolerance, economic development, technology and 'cultural pluralism' (Mee, 23) to create a unified nation that paved the way for the spirit of Indianness. A revived sense of a 'nation' (the one) and 'regions' (many and diverse) emerged, which contributed towards defining India as a unified country.

The concept of the nation was, in a sense, a prelude to the development of the theatre of roots. The performance practices from different regions of India were taken as a whole, out of which evolved 'a nationwide definition of Indian theatre', which exemplifies a notion of 'a larger Indian theatrical ethos' (Mee, 23). Mahatma Gandhi promoted traditional aesthetics of Indian culture. He spoke of 'creating a new society from the roots upwards' (Brown, 122). This idea, was reflected in the notion of 'swadeshi', which meant belonging to one's own country and boycotting the foreign goods in favour of Indian goods. For example, wearing 'Khadi' clothes and the use of 'charkha' became symbols of rejecting 'European values and their manifestation in criteria for decency' (Mee, 20).

After independence, the playwrights strove to re-present India nationally and internationally as a nation which upholds the legacy of legendary heroes, who decolonized the nation from the clutches of colonialism. The roots practitioners craved to create a theatre that would be genuinely Indian and could express "people's own cultural identity... [they] wanted to revitalize the stage by making it aesthetically relevant, with the knowledge that aesthetics are political" (Mee,74). The Indian people's Theatre Association (IPTA) which was established in the year 1942 prefigured the roots movement and shared common goals. For instance, both wanted theatre to express people's struggle for independence. Theatre was used as a political tool to outdo the British regime in India and the British authorities considered it as a 'potential threat to Empire' (Mee, 68). Playwrights depicted the atrocities inflicted by the British on the Indian masses which infused violent impulses among people. In the year 1876 the Dramatic Performances Act (DPA) was enacted to prohibit anti-colonial plays and the playwrights reverted to other themes.

The roots playwrights used legendary figures like Rani of Jhansi, Vasudeo Balwant Phadke, Tipu Sultan and Tughlaq — either to criticise the British Raj to make a political statement or to raise issues like caste discrimination, untouchability etc. Since the artists see India as 'an arena of cultural encounters', and also celebrate these encounters as creative and generative (Khilnani, xiv), the roots playwrights too, in spite of being rooted in culture, follow the tradition of celebrating the Indian- Mughal and Indian-British encounters in many ways. This is what can be defined as a new and alternative modernity. Decolonising the theatre, in essence, means incorporating all the historical changes that have affected the Indian mindset across ages.

Sometimes the theatre of roots is misunderstood as a movement propagating 'Hindu monoculture' (Nemichand Jain, quoted by Erin B.Mee,24), because of its insistence to resurrect the mythological past. However, this is a misconception. These playwrights, in spite of belonging to different regions of India, evoke the shared historical past of our country, besides mythology and folklore.

Girish Karnad incorporates major periods in the history of India, particularly the Mughal empire with an intention to endow his drama with a flavour that is uniquely Indian. He reconstructs the impact of the Mughal dynasties on the Indian culture and history. Karnad's dramatic genius lies in his extraordinary skill in using myth, history and folktales to carve out dramas enriched with thought provoking ideas, entailing gripping stories about our legendary heroes. At this juncture, it will not be out of place to note that eventually myths and history merge. In general usage, myth is often interchangeable with legend. Interpreted as a traditional story, a myth also embodies a justification for the early history of a society. It could be a story about 'a person or thing held in awe or generally referred to with near reverential admiration on the basis of popularly repeated stories 'Whether real or fictitious' (Wikipedia, 1).

Literature has its roots in history, past or present and thus every literary text is an outcome of a socio-historical environment. Karnad's plays are to be studied within a socio-historical perspective. In his introduction to *Three Plays* he acknowledges that history had an important framing influence on his works:

... tensions between the cultural past of the country and its colonial past, between the attractions of Western modes of thought and our own traditions, and finally between the various visions of the future... opened up once the common cause of political freedom was achieved. This is the historical context that gave rise to my plays and those of my contemporaries. (Karnad, Vol. 1)

The principle involved in combining myth and history is the preservation of tradition. The underlying idea is to discard the historical objectivism and to incorporate the idea of the aesthetic representation. History and myth eventually converge in Karnad's plays also. Myth strengthens the fictionality of the text and history justifies the claim of the text on the grounds of reality. Various thoughts and ideas conveyed are influenced by the historicity of an event. Just as there is fiction in myth, similarly representation of history involves attempts at fictionalizing it as well. History and myth, therefore, merge in contemporary literature. History gives us facts and yet it gets mingled with folk imagination. As and when history is re-incarnated it acquires a dimension which is no different from the mythic dimension. This lends a novel dimension to a literary text. The writer therefore, exploits a variety of literary devices so as to enrich the literariness of his writings. As Roman Jackbson puts it, "The subject of literary science is not literature, but literariness" (Wikipedia,3).

Karnad enriches his texts in various ways to represent history in a unique manner. He incorporates historical legends into his plays, uses them as stories about the past, which are based on some historical events. At the centre of these stories are generally human heroes. Just as myths explain the creation of the world and civilization, similarly, history too unravels the mysteries of cultural practices and the temper of the ages it belongs to. Both history and myths go a long way in determining the cultural and social patterns of societies of the world.

Myths and history, both refer to the past. Therefore, both have inextricable links. A myth refers to an indeterminate event having taken place in the remote past, that has a bearing on the present. In the same manner a historical event which has a concrete past also leads to many conditions which prevail currently. Karnad's drama represents a connection of the two:

The theme of tradition in Karnad's writings is given radical interpretation. ... Karnad explores the meaning of creativity by presenting a complex and provocatively ambiguous world, where fictional characters and real characters intermingle and the lines between the visible and invisible merge into each other spontaneously. What makes his work fascinating is that even though it is set in the traditional/folk or historical format, it examines issues that are contemporary. (Mansingh Chaudhry, The Tribune)

Reinterpreting *Tughlaq as* a Reflection of Modern Politics

One of the central issues surrounding the debate around the theatre of roots is its relevance to the present times. Attempts have been made to dismiss the theatre of roots as meaningless and irrelevant to the modern situation. The general assumption is that the theatre of roots cannot deal with the complexities of the modern world. "However one of the defining features of traditional performances is that they do not belong to the past: they are constantly reinventing themselves responding to contemporary political events and social changes, adapting to changing performance circumstances, and playing to new audiences" (Mee,27). Karnad's famous play *Tughlaq* has all the features that make it relevant to the modern times. *Tughlaq* is Karnad's second play which was published in 1964. It was first produced in Kannada in 1965 and at the same time it was performed in Hindi by the National School of Drama.

The play explores the paradox of the idealistic Sultan Muhammad-bin-Tughlaq, whose reign is considered as one of the most notable in India's history. *Tughlaq* is a historical play, where Karnad "reconstructs history and recreates it imaginatively" (Vashishtha, Web, 3). Karnad has well searched the chosen period of Indian history and with little changes, he has introduced both historical and fictional characters.

Karnad in his play presents an amalgam of rich and complex symbolism blended with different motifs. The play has an interesting story and an intricate plot which supposedly parallels the political mood of disillusionment that followed the post-independence era of idealism in the country. Karnad himself has commented on this:

What struck me absolutely about Tughlaq's history was that it was contemporary. The fact that here was the most idealistic, the most intelligent King ever to come on the throne of Delhi... and one of the greatest failures also. And within a span of twenty years this tremendously capable man had gone to pieces... due to his idealism as well as the shortcomings within him, such as his impatience, his cruelty, his feeling that he had the only correct answer. And I felt in the early sixties India had also come very far in the same direction - the twenty-year period seemed to me much a striking parallel. (Karnad, viii)

Karnad uses the legendary King Muhammad-bin-Tughlaq to bring out the historical as well as contemporary political scenario to the fore. The play is "contemporary in the sense that one can see flashes of 'Tughlaqi' attitude callous yet well-meaning in contemporary political structures too" (Vashistha, Web, 2). The play deals with various issues. On one hand, it depicts a character who is all intelligent, immensely powerful, blessed with all skills, but is still a failure as far as his capability to reign a kingdom is concerned. Karnad uses this enigmatic figure to portray as to how even absolute power is doomed to failure. Karnad's play shows the transformation of the character, the medieval ruler Mohammad-bin-Tughlaq from a sensitive and intelligent ruler who sets out to do the best for his people into a tyrant. He is misunderstood and maligned, suffers from an acute sense of alienation and is forced to abandon this idealism. In a way this becomes a negative transformation. The play can, thus, be seen as a tale of an over-ambitious, yet considerably virtuous king whose dreams and aspirations came to nought.

The character of Tughlaq has been endowed with specific ambiguities. The rest of the characters in the play are "dramatized aspects of his complex personality, yet they also exist in their own right" (Karnad, viii). The play relates the character of Tughlaq to philosophical issues of human nature. Reminiscent of Shakespeare's Richard II, he is more of a dreamer than a man of action.

Tughlaq also deals with the tragedy of "the limits of human power in a predominantly psychological context. This theme of human power is explored by Karnad in respect of a self-righteous idealist king wielding absolute power over his subjects." (Vashishtha, web, 3). The play has a didactic appeal as well, in the Brechtian sense. In his introduction to the play Karnad has mentioned very clearly that "the play is more than a political allegory. It has an irreducible, puzzling quality which comes from the ambiguities of Tughlaq's character, the dominating figure in the play" (Karnad, viii). The play, opens in the yard in front of the Chief Court of Justice in Delhi. A large number of people, are gathered in the yard, 'mostly Muslims, with a few Hindus'. In the crowd there is an old man who seems worried about the country's future and exclaims, "God, what's this country coming to!" (Karnad, Tughlaq, 1).

A young man assures him that the country is in safe hands. From their conversation, however, is apparent people's scepticism about Sultan's ability. Religion is apparently important to the Sultan. The Muslims are annoyed because Tughlaq has exempted the Hindus from the payment of Jaziya Tax, which they always paid. Tughlaq has also made it mandatory to pray five times a day, as ordained in the Koran. Karnad brings out the character of Tughlaq through the conversations between the characters, before Tughlaq appears on the scene.

The public announcer then beats drums calling for attention and we are told that the land of a Brahmin, Vishnu Prasad was seized illegally by the officers of the state. He had filed a suit against His Merciful Majesty, that he should be given just compensation for the loss of the land and the privation resulting there from. The Kazi-i-Mumalik has declared that the Brahmin's claim is just and His Majesty (Tughlaq) is guilty of illegal appropriation of land. The confiscated land would be returned to him along with a grant of five hundred silver dinars. In addition to this, he would also get a post in the Civil Service. The Announcer beats the drum again and then appears Tughlaq followed by the Kazi.

The Announcer once again calls for attention:

Attention! Attention! The Warrior in the Path of God, the Defender of the word of the Prophet, the Friend of the Khalif, the Just, His Merciful Majesty, Sultan Muhammad Tughlaq.(3)

Muhammad's address to his people has echoes of a public speech of any present day leader before elections. The tone is rhetorical, the claims exaggerated and the vision of future grandiose:

Muhammad: My beloved people, you have heard the judgement of the Kazi and seen for yourselves how justice works in my Kingdom without any consideration of might or weakness, religion or creed. May this moment burn bright and light up our path towards greater justice, equality, progress and peace - not just peace but a more purposeful life. (30)

Karnad incorporates the actual historical details, inviting the audience to react. More often than not the reaction of the audience appears to be the same as that of public in the play itself. Tughlaq's erratic nature is foregrounded as he further asks for support and cooperation to achieve this end and abruptly announces that the capital of his empire will be moved from Delhi to Daulatabad. The crowd reacts in bewilderment and Muhammad smiles. He tries to justify his decision by saying that this has been decided after careful thought and discussion and that 'this is no mad whim of a tyrant'. Seeing public's perplexity, it actually appears to be exactly a mad man's sudden fancy. He explains that Delhi being near the border is threatened by the invaders and his empire is large now and needs a capital at its heart. Like a strategic politician, he further adds that "for me the most important factor is that Daulatabad is a city of the Hindus and as the capital it will symbolize the bond between Muslims and Hindus which I wish to develop and strengthen in my Kingdom". He expresses his desire to build 'an empire which will be the envy of the World'. He invites people to accompany him to Daulatabad and says that it is not an order, it is an invitation.

The play highlights how people begin to cash in on rulers' populist policies, weaknesses and eccentricities. The real beneficiaries of such policies are seldom the ones who deserve the benefits. It is always the manipulative and the scheming, who end up reaping the advantage. As Guard disperses the crowd shouting at them to go home as "The show's over!" (5), Only Aazam hangs behind as he wants to see who the Brahmin is. The Brahmin turns out to be his close friend Aziz, whom he had not met for a long time. Aziz is disguised as a Brahmin from whom he had bought the land. Aziz reminds Azam about the royal proclamation according to which people can file a suit against the Sultan for any misbehaviour of his officers and that justice will be done. Aziz, who is basically a dhobi sees no future in being a dhobi and, therefore, disguises himself as a Hindu Brahmin for whom the Sultan would do justice. Aziz sarcastically comments that if he would have come dressed up as a Muslim it would be a "Muslim plaintiff against a Muslim King" (8). Now Aziz has acquired a government position and invites Aazam to come with him and work as his subordinate.

Karnad refers to the comic pair of Akara and Makara of *Natak* performances from where he drew inspiration to create the comic pair of Aziz and Aazam. The theatre audiences respond readily to such comic pairs, who assume various disguises and provide fun and humour imparting dramatic relief. These characters make witty but pertinent remarks on the situations, mostly in satiric vein.

The play brings to the fore Tughlaq's ambitious nature as well as idealism through incidents such as the one concerning the so called poor Brahmin. He has been portrayed as a ruler, who misses no opportunity to show off his lofty ideals. When his stepmother asks him as to what does he do all night. In a theatrical manner he replies:

I pray to the Almighty to save me from sleep. All day long I have to worry about tomorrow, but it's only when the night falls that I can step beyond all that... I want to climb up, up to the top of the tallest tree in the World, and call out to my people. 'Come, my people, I am waiting for you. Confide in me your worries. Let me share your joys. Let's laugh and cry together and then let's pray. Let's pray till our bodies melt and flow and our blood turns into air. History is ours to play with-our now! Let's be the light and cover earth with greenery. Let's be darkness and cover up the boundaries of nations. Come! I am waiting to embrace you all!'(10)

Tughlaq's desire to climb the tallest tree and calling his people to confide their worries in him reflects his urge to be an ideal King. His alienated self is depicted here as he calls out to his people to pray till their blood turns into air. History is important for Tughlaq as he wants to be remembered as a great King. He also appears to fail in his attempt to communicate with his people. He further adds in a flamboyant style, which becomes his characteristic manner in the course of the play:

But then how can I spread my branches in the stars while the roots have yet to find their hold in the earth? I wish I could believe in recurring births like the Hindu but I have only one life, one body, and my hopes, my people, my God are all fighting for it. Tell me, how dare I waste my time by sleeping? And don't tell me to go and get married and breed a family because I won't sleep. (10)

Tughlaq's fears, hopes and dreams are very clearly brought out through this monologue. Karnad has brilliantly delineated the character of Tughlaq. The audiences can relate to his character and empathize with him. The play has immense relevance to the modern situation because it provides the idealism of post-independence era in India, when high-sounding promises were made by those who were at the helm of affairs. However, what followed the lofty idealism was a mood of utter disillusionment.

Karnad highlights Tughlaq's dilemmas that have always dogged him. By implication, the play also underscores how rulers, since times immemorial, have indulged in crimes such as parricide and fratricide in order to serve their ends. The issue of morality of these acts is pushed to the background for the sake of an overvaulting ambition. Tughlaq is worried because Sheikh Imam-ud-din (who is turning the people in Kanpur against him) and his friend Ain-ul-Mulk have revolted and are marching towards Delhi with an army of thirty thousand soldiers and Muhammad hardly has six thousand soldiers to fight against him. We are introduced to Barani and Nazib. According to Tughlaq "Barani is a historian - he's only interested in playing chess with the shadows of the dead. And Nazib's a politician - he wants pawns of flesh and blood" (12). The sultan is also aware that Sheikh Imam-ud-din has been telling people that Tughlaq is a murderer, who has killed his father and brother at prayer time. Even Muhammad questions Barani "Do you really think parricide is a little thing? And Fratricide? And the pollution of prayer? (13). Tughlaq's persistent questioning brings to the surface his guilt and while he seems to put this question to Barani, he actually directs it at himself.

Karnad also suggests how the morally upright and the courageous amongst us always have to pay the price for speaking up against injustice. Muhammad's next move in the play of power game is his invitation to Sheikh Imam-ud-din, his worst critic, to address a meeting of the people where the Sultan himself would also be present. The Announcer calls for attention. As directed by Tughlaq the announcer also adds that the Sheikh "will analyse His Merciful Majesty's administration" and show where he has "inadvertently taken wrong measures..." (18). The Sheikh has been reported to have said that Muhammad has forfeited the right to rule by murdering his father and brother during prayer time, thereby polluting the prayer. Tughlaq arranges things in such a way that not a single person turns up for the meeting. The Sheikh is, thus, disgraced and is declared as a spy. Imam-ud-din is disappointed and points out 'scores of transgressions' on

Muhammad's part and accuses him of having put the best of Ulemas and Sayyids behind bars in the name of justice. Muhammad, however, defends himself:

They tried to indulge in politics - I couldn't allow that... there is dirt and sickness in my kingdom. But why should I call on God to clean the dirt deposited by men? (20)

Imam-ud-din wants to make him realise that only the Voice of God, the Holy Word can do it. He says that the Arabs spread Islam for seven hundred years and now Tughlaq should take the lead. He stresses the point and says:

You could do it. You are one of the most powerful Kings on earth today and you could spread the Kingdom of Heaven on earth. God has given you everything - power, learning, intelligence, talent. Now you must repay His debt.(20)

Karnad points to the overvaulting ambition of Tughlaq: "I have a long way to go. I can't afford to crawl. I have to gallop" (20). Immam-ud-din accuses Muhammad of trying to become God:

Beware Sultan, you are trying to become another God. It's a sin worse than parricide... Religion! Politics! Take heed, Sultan, one day such verbal distinctions will rip you into two. (21)

Tughlaq emerges as a scheming politician who scares the Sheikhs that people in Delhi consider him as a spy as no one turned up to listen to him. He says that Sheikh has risked his life by speaking against the Sultan. Muhammad's masterstroke in power-politics is yet to come. He persuades Sheikh to go as his envoy to meet Ain-ul-Mulk to dissuade him from marching to Delhi. The bait is that such a saintly person would not like to see Muslims slaughtered at the hands of fellow Muslims. Tughlaq says:

I am willing to make peace but how can I do it? I don't even know why he has turned against me. He won't even see my official envoys. But he will see you. He respects you as every muslim in India does. He will trust your word (23).

Tughlaq traps Sheikh Imam-ud-din into believing his words. The Sheikh who resembles Tughlaq is given royal robes and is put on the royal elephant. The meeting is set near the plains of Kannauj. The soldiers led by Ain-ul-Mulk think it is Tughlaq coming for peace talks. Tughlaq's soldiers start the attack as a trumpet is sounded as a signal for attack. Soldiers attack Ain-ul-Mulk's army, as they pour out from behind the surrounding hills. Sheikh Imam-ud-din is killed and Ain-ul-Mulk's army rushes in the trap set by Tughlaq. It was the 'bloodiest massacre' ever seen, says Rattan Singh, an eyewitness in the play.

The play is a powerful comment on the way the mighty kings make the mistake of donning the mantle of god himself. There is a subtle but certain suggestion on the similar conduct of the modern politicians, who think they are invincible and can indulge in almost everything to ensure their place in power politics. The political intrigue of Tughlaq has a strong parallel in the present-day political setup. The game of chess is used symbolically by Karnad to highlight certain important aspects in the play. Tughlaq won the battle with Ain-ul-Mulk because of Sheikh Imam-ud-din who is killed mistakenly. Tughlaq shows his generosity by pardoning Ain-ul-Mulk as he could detect a flaw in a problem already being solved by the Sultan. "I had spent days on that wretched problem and he spots a flaw within half a minute" (28). For Tughlaq a game of chess has become a game of power, of power politics, where to survive is more important rather than the means by which one survives. For Tughlaq killing the Sheikh was more important and Ain-ul-Mulk indirectly helped him. The Sultan thus emerges victorious and pardons his friend. Karnad seems to suggest that the scheming politicians, who occupy the echelons of power, can go any length, when it comes to serving their own interest. Even the good men are corrupted by the charm of wielding power. *Tughlaq* .therefore, has immense relevance for the modern times as well. Because in the character of Tughlaq is mirrored the intrigue of the present day politicians. The play, therefore, can be seen as a parable for political intrigue.

The play also focuses on the discontent that eventually builds up against the rulers. No community can ever be satisfied wholly by those at the helm of affairs. If the ruler is kind to one community, the other half feels neglected and vice-versa. A similar situation unfolds in *Tughlaq* too. Amir believes that the Sultan wants to weaken the Amirs as they are strong in Delhi and it is Sultan's strategy to shift the capital to Daulatabad because the Hindus have a strong hold there. The Sheikh shows his concern for Islam:

Haven't you heard what's happening to the leaders of Islam today? Sheikh Haidari is in prison. Sheikh Hood in exile... Is it a crime to speak out for oneself and one's family! What politics did Sheikh Imam-ud-din indulge in? That he was open, frank and honest? (32)

Sheikh also reveals that the day when Imam-ud-din was to address the people:

... on that very afternoon, soldiers went from door to door threatening dire consequences if anyone dared to attend the meeting. (33)

The Sheikh unbuttons his shirt and shows a wound on his shoulder, he says:

I tried to force my way to the Big Mosque and this is what I got for it... (33)

The play is a powerful commentary on the political intrigues and conspiracies that have been there since times immemorial. Ratan Singh reveals another fact that Shihab-ud-din's father killed Ratan Singh's father through treachery and usurped the Kingdom. To atone for his father's sin, Shihab-ud-din treats Ratan Singh as his adopted brother. Shihab-ud-din is trapped by Ratan Singh to be part of the conspiracy to kill Tughlaq. Ratan Singh says that at prayer time soldiers are not allowed to carry arms and thus the palace is unarmed. They decide that next Tuesday when the Amirs will be seeing the Sultan for the Durbar-i-Khas, they would attack the Sultan. "The muezzin's call to prayer will be the signal of attack!" (35).

The Sheikh expresses his dissent by sayings that it is not right to pollute the sacred time of prayer, but Amir-II replies mockingly, "... we can make up later. Do penance for it"(36).Girish Karnad never misses an opportunity to have a dig at the hypocrisy and pseudo-veneer of the so called guardians of religion. Muhammad-bin- Tughlaq himself is not unaffected by it. On learning that the descendants of the last Khalif is visiting the capital, he comments:

A visit by the descent of the Khalif could show how faithful I am or how religious I am or even perhaps how modest... (38)

Tughlaq's words reflect his religious and moral dilemma. The playwright seems to suggest that what may appear to be the hypocritical veneer of Tughlaq can indeed be his guilty conscience. He says that he has been questioning himself since Sheikh Imam-ud-din died that "... what gives me the right to call myself a King? Am I a King only because I am the son of a King? Or is it because I can make the people accept my laws and the army move to my commands? ... I ask you - all of you - what would you have me do to become a real King in your eyes?" (38)

The situation foregrounds his deepest fears and anxieties. He is aware that he lacks the trust and confidence of his people. He also knows that to be a 'real king', one needs to have greater commitment and nobility. He accepts the fact that he is not happy : "But I am not happy and I am turning to tradition and history now and seeking an answer there..." (38-39) Tradition and history provide solutions to many complexities of modern day existence. By making this statement, Tughlaq echoes the predicament of many great men in history. His conscience torments him: "How can I explain tomorrow to those who haven't even opened their eyes to the light of today?" (39)

Tughlaq's desperation after assessing that his people will not easily accept his reforms, howsoever well-meaning, assumes tragic proportions. After his suggestion to introduce copper coins along with silver dinars is met with resistance, Muhammad begs them to trust him and support him as he hopes of building a new future for India. He kneels down before them which embarrasses everyone present there. Shihab-ud-din says:

Yours Majesty, it's not for a King to beg. He must command. We are your ever-willing servants. (40)

Muhammad then asks everyone that, if it is so then all should take an oath on the Koran to support him in all his measures. The door-keeper then informs that it's the hour of prayer. Muhammad stands silent in the tense atmosphere and then says "We'll all pray here" (41). As the Muezzin's call begins, everyone start praying, taking that as a cue, Shihab-ud-din and the Amirs get up and pull out their daggers to attack the Sultan. Barani is frightened at this. As the Amir steps towards the throne to attack Tughlaq, about twenty Hindu soldiers rush in with spears from behind the curtain and surround the Amirs. One or two Amirs try to run out but the soldiers bar their way. The Amirs stand frozen in fear and throw their daggers. Only Shihab-ud-din is left and others are dragged away by the soldiers. While all this is going on, Muhammad goes on praying as if totally unconcerned. He steps down from the throne only when he finishes praying. Muhammad tells Shibab-ud-din that a letter was written by Ratan Singh to the Sultan by which

Muhammad got to know about this plan. Ratan Singh has disappeared after taking his revenge upon Shihab-ud-din.

Tughlaq asks Shihab-ud-din as to what wrong has he done to him and why did he plan to kill him. Shihab gets violent and tells Muhammad - "Get on with your killing, Muhammad... But you can't stop this uprising now" (42). He says that through letters he has reported all these cruel happenings at Muhammad's Kingdom to his father who distrusts him. Muhammad says that all those letters have been sent by Ratan Singh to the Sultan. Shihab-ud-din screams and questions Muhammad "Where will you hide my corpse? How will you gag my voice?" (43) Muhammad almost in a frenzy goes on stabbing him and hits out at Shihab-ud-din's dead body with a ferocity that even the soldiers holding the body recoil in horror. Barani tells him - 'Majesty - he's dead!' Muhammad then flings the dagger away in disgust. Deeply anguished and almost insane now, he asks Barani:

Why must this happen. Are all those I trust condemned to go down in history as traitors? ... Will my reign be nothing more than a tortured scream... (43)

He orders that every man involved in this be caught and beheaded, their bodies to be stuffed with straw and taken round the Kingdom. However, he makes as a smart move as a political leader, he knows how to turn the situation to his advantage. He says:

Make a public announcement that there was a rebellion in the palace and that the nobles of the court tried to assassinate the Sultan during prayer... (43)

Tughlaq is presented as a vindictive ruler, out to annihilate his detractors. At the same time he comes across as a manipulator. He asks his soldiers to say that the Sultan was saved by Shihab-ud-din who died a martyr's death defending him. His funeral will be a grand affair and Shihab's father is invited to it and is to be treated with the respect due to the father of a loyal nobleman. To this Barani replies "Oh God! Aren't even the dead free from your politics?" (43-44).

Karnad highlights the inherent insecurities of a ruler, who does not hesitate to perpetrate cruelty after cruelty on the unsuspecting subjects, while he justifies his actions. Tughlaq becomes absolutely heartless and despondent. At the same time, he is tormented by his conscience. Banning prayers throughout the kingdom, he says in utter desperation:

Not a light should be seen in the windows of Delhi. Not a wisp of smoke should rise from its chimneys. Nothing but an empty graveyard of Delhi will satisfy me now. (44)

Karnad powerfully underscores not just the unrelenting cruelty of Tughlaq but also the shock of having been attacked in prayer, that has driven him to near insanity. He is utterly distraught and begins to suspect every act of prayer:

I had wanted every act in my Kingdom to become a prayer, every prayer to become a further step in knowledge, further step to lead us nearer to God. But our prayers too are ridden with disease... Henceforth let the moment of prayer walk by streets in silence and leave without a trace (44).

U.R. Anantha Murthy in the Introduction to the play writes that Karnad makes use of 'prayer' as the leitmotif of the play, in the scene where the Muslim Chieftans along with Sheikh-Shams-ud-din, a pacificist priest, conspire to murder Tughlaq while at prayer. The use of prayer for murder reminds us of what Tughlaq himself had done to kill his father.

That prayer, which is most dear to Tughlaq, is vitiated by him as well as his enemies, is symbolic of the fact that his life is corrupted at its very source, (ix)

The whole incident is ironic. It involves Shihab-ud-din, an idealist who has put great trust in Tughlaq's rule but he is ultimately betrayed by Ratan Singh who masterminds the entire plan of murder to serve his own ends.

The intrigue here not only enhances the theatrical interest of the play, but is a dramatized projection of Tughlaq's tortured, divided self, (ix)

Karnad invariably attacks dogmatic approach to religion. He places greater emphasis on the values of compassion and love that dogmatic attitudes do not necessarily subscribe to. This is clearly borne out by an incident from the play. As people leave Delhi for Daulatabad as per Sultan's commands, many lives perish en route either of disease or starvation. There is a kind man, who on seeing two corpses lying unattended on the road is moved and gives them a burial. The comic pair of Azam and Aziz is also present there. Aziz who is disguised as a Hindu Brahmin questions the kind man's motives: "what if they were Hindus...I ought to send you back to dig them up again. It's against the orders to insult or cause harm to Hinduism"(48).The cutting edge of Karnad's irony becomes even sharper as the man announces he is a kafir and his job was to protect dead bodies. In the palace yard, in order to save the tax, Sultan had imposed tax on the relatives to take away their dead, even "the rich folk—the most respectable people of Delhi" would steal the dead bodies. The whole episode acquires significance in the present day context, as the rich and the respectable people of society are as adept at evading taxes as anyone else. Karnad's satiric intent is clearly visible in his portrayal of this episode.

Tughlaq, therefore, transcends limits of historical time. The political intrigue is a timeless fact. The scheming, unscrupulous and heartless people are generally in command regardless of the age they belong to. In spite of being set in a remote time and space, the play is extremely relevant to the modern times as it presents the treachery, cruelty and intrigue underlying the political set up in any age. Aziz's comment is highly pertinent in this regard:

... Only a few months in Delhi and I have discovered a whole new world - politics! My dear fellow, that's where our future is - politics! It is a beautiful world - wealth, success, position, power - and yet it's full of brainless people, people with not an idea in their head. (50)

The political scenario in the present times is also quite similar. The politicians use all kinds of tricks to gain wealth, power and position to secure their position in the echelons of power. In contemporary world the game of power politics is as dark and manipulative as it was in the times of Tughlaq. Aziz and Aazam visualise a secure future in this kind of politics. They make a lot of money by getting bribes and thrive on the suffering of the people. Aziz being the office incharge and Aazam as his follower are tired of their being small time rogues and decide to make money in a big way. They plan to make counterfeit copper coins and exchange them for silver coins, which will be in accordance with the orders of the Sultan.

The play becomes quite reflective towards the end. Muhammad- bin - Tughlaq typifies an alienated ruler, whose dreams of building a strong empire have ended in a fiasco. However, he is wiser now. Though it is already too late and all that Tughlaq can recount are his failures:

... I shall build my own history like this, brick by brick... One night I was standing on the ramparts of the old fort. There was a torch near me flapping its wild wings and scattering golden feathers on everything in sight. There was a half-built gate nearby trying to contain the sky within its cleft. Suddenly something happened as though some one had cast a spell. The torch, the gate, the fort and the sky- all melted and merged and flowed in my blood-stream with the darkness of the night. (53)

This speech is highly symbolic. The python can be taken to be a symbol of Tughlaq's barbarity, inhumanity and brutality. The torch and the gate symbolize Tughlaq's failure, as the gate is half built and the torch is the torch of knowledge, which he wanted to spread amongst his people. The final melting of the torch, the gate, the fort and the sky into the darkness of night suggest that all his hopes and dreams have been dashed to ground and there is eternal darkness, fear and confusion that surround him now. As he puts it:

The moment shed its symbols, its questions and answers, and stood naked and calm where the stars throbbed in my veins. I was the earth, was the grass, was the smoke, was the sky. Suddenly a sentry called from far... [and] the half-burnt torch and the half-built gate fell apart.(53)

Tughlaq also tells the young man that in the last four years he has seen only the woods clinging to the earth and heard only the howl of wild wolves and dogs. Five years ago he used to pray to God not to send him any sleep and now he needs a peaceful sleep but does not get it. As a ruler his troubles are multiplying, Bahal-ud-din Gashtasp has raised army against Tughlaq; there is draught in Doab and the only industry that flourishes in his kingdom is of making counterfeit copper coins.

At this stage of life, it dawns on Tughlaq that he is disliked as a king by his subjects and they are now waiting for him to close his eyes. Karnad's king can be compared to any idealist ruler, who had the best of intentions but lacked farsightedness and vision to translate them into reality. His dejection, guilt and inner turmoil make him a picture of grief: "The only way I can abdicate is by killing myself (56). He further says:

I could have done something if the vultures weren't so close. I would have crawled forward on my knees and elbows... every moment you expect a beak to dig into you and tear a muscle out? What can you do? Barani, what vengeance is driving these shapes after me? (56)

Karnad uses the birds of prey symbolically. Tughlaq's spiritual anguish and agony are brought to the fore with the use of the symbol of vulture, which can be linked to the torments of conscious he suffers from. His pain is unremitting. He is also aware that his beloved subjects call him Mad Muhammad. He asks Barani how can he become wise again. He accepts that all these years he has been in the wrong :

I have something to give, something to teach, which may open the eyes of history, but I have to do it within this life. I've got to make them listen to me before I lose even that!(56)

Barani reminds him of the bloodshed, torture for the smallest offence and hanging people on grounds of suspicion—atrocities that have been rampant in his empire. Barani pleads with him to stop all this. He also reminds him that there was a time when Tughlaq believed in love, in peace and in God. He asks him to regain those ideals.

It is at this time that Muhammad is informed that Muhammad Najib has been murdered. To add to his frustration he comes to know that it is his own step-mother who had poisoned Najib. She believed that Najib had been misguiding the Sultan. The stepmother confesses to having poisoned Vizir Najib, Muhammad is totally shattered by now and tells her that "There's only one punishment for treachery - death!" (66). Muhammad orders that she be prisoned and stoned to death for adultery. Muhammad is heart-broken and prays:

God, God in Heaven please help me... My skin drips with blood and I don't know how much of it is mine and how much of others. I started in Your path, Lord, ... I started in search of You. Why am I become a pig rolling in this gory mud? Raise me. Clean me. Cover me with your Infinite Mercy. I can only beg - have pity on me. I have no one but you now. Only You. Only You... You... You... You.. .(67)

There is deep irony in the way public prayers are resumed as soon as Ghias-ud-din arrives. It is, in fact, Aziz who is disguised as Ghias-ud-din. Once again there is a scathing attack on dogmas. Everyone is starving. The people want food not prayers. "Prayer! Prayer! Who wants prayers now? Ask them to give us some food"(70).

The roads are lined with skeletons, people are eating barks off the trees. They are begging for "just a fistful of rice - a piece of meat..." (72). Some asking to be killed rather than starve. When the soldiers try to subside the voices, they are attacked and thus riots begin in Daultabad and people are killed in thousands. There are many references in the play which point the utter disillusionment of Tughlaq as he is on the brink of insanity. He spent years planning that rose garden, the idea of which is a mere trapping now:

Now I don't need a rose garden. I built it because I wanted to make for myself an image of Sadi's poems. I wanted every rose in it to be a poem. I wanted every thorn in it to prick and quicken the senses. But I don't need these airy trappings now, a funeral has no need for a separate symbol.(63-64)

The symbolism of the above speech is important, Muhammad wanted to build an empire which would have been the envy of the world. He wanted to inculcate the principles of justice, quality, peace and progress leading towards a more purposeful life. In a similar vein, he expected every flower in his garden to blossom and portray an image of Sadi's poem. But the reality turned out to be different.

In a final and 'mad' decision, Tughlaq decides to shift the capital back to Delhi, still not sure of whether he is doing the right or is in the wrong.

I don't know if I am pursuing a mirage or fleeting a shadow... all I need now is myself and my madness.. I have a companion to share my madness now - the Omnipotent God! (85)

Tired and exhausted the Sultan falls asleep on the throne. At the time of public prayer a servant tries to awaken him, but goes out without doing so. The play ends with Muhammad looking around dazed and frightened as though he cannot comprehend where he is.

Tughlaq, the idealistic ruler who ascended his throne (by usurpation) with an idea to "centralize administration" and with his Utopian idea of a unified India, failed in his endeavour to do so. The play has the grandeur of a classic. The structure is compact and creates the effect of a unified whole. The incidents and situations coordinate with characters. They have their basis in the self-contradictory actions of the protagonist. The symbolism of the game of chess, the theme of disguise, the ironic success of Aziz whose story runs parallel to Tughlaq's are skilfully used by Karnad to bring out the binary opposition between the man and the hero in Tughlaq, which is the source of the entire tragedy.

Karnad is thoroughly acquainted with historical details. In one of his observations on the play, he says that to be mad was very much fashionable at a time when he wrote this play. As he started reading about Tughlaq, Karnad realised what a fantastic character he was and the legendary King Muhammad-bin-Tughlaq came alive to him.

The traditional sources present a somewhat prejudiced and biased view of the life and times of Tughlaq. Muhammad is known to be the most misunderstood monarch of his time. Tughlaq's idealism, his visionary temperament, religious tolerance and a rationalistic view is in close affirmation to the historical facts. The paradoxes and contradictions emerge as the central trait of this legendary king. In the introduction to the play, Ananth Murthy points out:

... the external action throughout enacts the inner drama of Tughlaq. Both Tughlaq and his enemies initially appear to be idealists; yet, in the pursuit of the ideal, they perpetrate its opposite. The whole play is structured on these opposites, the ideal and the real, the divine aspiration and the deft intrigue, (ix)

Tughlaq has been regarded as a contemporary play about a contemporary situation. Having a parallel with the present day political intrigues and shallow idealism, the play powerfully articulates the intricacies of power politics in the context of the present day political situation.

Tale-Danda and the Contemporary Politics of Divisibility

The thematic concerns of *Tale-Danda* are different from those of Karnad's earlier plays. The play traces the history of religious uprising in India which later took forms of 'secularization and fundamentalism' (Dharwadker, x). Karnad once again turns to the history of medieval India, to re-present the contemporary socio-religious aspects which dominate the mainstream India even today.

The play's historical narrative centres on the twelfth-century religious movement Virasaivism, a reform and protest movement, led by the poet Saint Basavanna. The movement flourished in the city of Kalyan (the present day Karnataka) for a short period of time under the Kingship of Bijjala, and subsequently ended in violence and bloodshed. In the play *Tale-Danda,* Karnad highlights certain aspects which are related to the caste-system prevalent in our society. With the rituals and traditions forming the backdrop of the play, Karnad focuses on the central issues such as caste conflict, class divisions, limitations and boundaries of the caste system within the Hindu society. In the preface to the play, he mentions that he wrote the play in 1989 'when the Mandir and Mandal movements were beginning to show again how relevant the questions posed by these thinkers (the Virsaivas) were for our age. The horror of subsequent events and the religious fanaticism that has gripped our national life today have only proved how dangerous it is to ignore the solutions they offered' (Dharwadker, xii).

The play has been set during the two decades ending in AD 1168, in the city of Kalyan where lived Basavanna. He mobilized a congregation of poets, mystics, social revolutionaries and philosophers to lead a movement called 'Virsaivism'. The movement aimed at uprooting the caste system in Hindu society. The idea was to propagate freedom of thought and devotional value based worship, thereby rejecting idol worship. The followers of this movement known as 'Sharanas', came in conflict with the orthodox upper-caste sections of society. As Aparna Dharwadker comments:

The Virasaiva communitarians ... exchanged the boundaries of caste for the bonds of friendships, fellowship, equality, humanity and social change. (Dharwadker, xi)

The ancient law givers refer to four recognised classes called 'Varnas' amongst the Hindus —Brahmins (which includes priests, poets, teachers and ministers), Vaishyas (tradesmen), Sudras (craftsmen) and the Panchamas (menial workers). Shudras and Panchamas toil and produce wealth which people of higher classes enjoy. According to a Hindu myth these four recognised classes emanated respectively from the mouth, the arms, the thighs and the feet of Lord Brahma, the creator . The 'Karma' theory also plays an important part in this supposedly rationalistic division. 'Karma', the action as in the *Bhagvadgita* or 'Karma', the profession as is in the literal sense, offer a significant explanation.

A Brahmin could change his 'Karma' (profession) and become a Kshatriya, a Vaishya or Shudra by caste conversion. Later, in the eleventh century A.D. the concept of 'Karma' was replaced and importance was given to one's caste in which one was born. A Brahmin or a Shudra had to live in the same caste in which he was born. They were forced to follow the profession of their forefathers. The dramatic structure of the play centres around King Bijjala, whose forefathers converted themselves to Kshatriyas, who found acceptance in the society among the sharanas.

The sharanas defined caste in a different way. They related the concept of caste to a mind set, which can be separated from the body and counterbalanced through reasoning. It is this conflict of mind and body and the resulting irony which forms the core of the play.

Among the greatest influences that shaped *Tale-Danda* were the discussions, Karnad had with A.K. Ramanujan. *Speaking of Siva* (1973), an anthology which consists of translations of the free verse lyrics of Basavanna, also went a long way in giving the play its present form. *Tale-Danda* literally means death by beheading, 'Tale', a Kannada word means 'Head' and Danda refers to punishment, that is inflicted on head. In medieval Karnataka it was a common practice to offer one's head either on the completion of a vow or in penitence. Saint Basavanna who actually lived in that period, uses the word quite often in the play.

Basavanna, heads the Virsaivism movement and spends his time preaching his fellow followers. "... [T]he figure of Basavanna [is] ... psychologically complex, historically plausible, and theatrically sustainable"(xv). Not only the character of Basavanna is endowed with above traits, but he can also be seen as a revolutionary figure in many ways. Karnad presents this character as an embodiment of the spirit of modernity. As pointed out earlier, Karnad sets many of his plays in remote historic time and space, yet they emerge extremely relevant to the modern situation. Like *Tughlaq, Tale- Danda* too is a powerful comment on the way power structures operate in society. The disparities between the upper and lower castes, the class conflicts, coupled with violence against the marginalised are among many topical issues that the play deals with.

Like most revolutionaries, Basavanna becomes the bane of those, who want to perpetuate class and caste hierarchy. Young people, who are his followers and work for the social causes are not accepted by society. People accuse him of enticing the youth:

Why can't that Basavanna see some sense? In every household in Kalyan, it's the same story. Father against son-brother against brother. (Karnad, Vol. 2, 8)

Not only are the ordinary people in the towns disgruntled but the signs of protest become apparent even in the rural households. The king Bijjala's trust in Basavana is absolute, whom he has made the finance minister. This is not tolerated by his son, Sovideva whom the king refers to as 'royal eunuch' and 'a bumpkin'. Sovideva bursts out in anger:

I am the Yuvraj of the Kalachurya dynasty - and those louts have the insolence to make a fool of me in front of the whole city? (14)

Basavanna, in a sense, represents the voice of the new generation. He is synonymous with change. Bijjala, the king, who is a barber by caste obviously finds a great and vocal supporter in Basvanna. Girish Karnad's play is a contemptuous attack on the inherent evil of the caste system. In a subtle way, he also highlights the desperate attempts made across ages by people to convert to higher castes in order to gain respectability. As Bijjala, the king comments:

... I am Bijjala the Emperor of Kalyan, the strong-shouldered Kalachurya conquerer! And yet-what is my caste? ... you may be Kshatriyas. But I am a Kalachurya, Katta churra, A barber. His Majesty King Bijjala is a barber by caste. (20-21)

He further adds that for ten generations his forefathers made several efforts to convert into Kashtriyas. They married into every royal family, bribed generations of Brahmins with millions of cows, so that they could get Kshatriyas branded on their foreheads. The sardonic irony of Bijjala's comment is too unambiguous to be missed. It reflects the way the hegemonic orders have always perpetuated caste hierarchy :

One's caste is like the skin on one's body. You can peel it off top to toe, but when the new skin forms, there you are again: a barber - a shepherd - a scavenger! (21)

For Bijjala being human is more important. He believes that only Basavanna and his men treat him as 'a human being' without referring to his 'lowly birth'. The King respects Basavanna who has inspired poets, mystics and visionaries. Bijjala also supports Basavanna in his mission 'to eradicate the caste structure, wipe it off the face of the earth. Annihilate the varna system'. Bijjala praises Basavanna and his people.

What a vision! And what prodigious courage! And he has the ability... [The Sharnas are] All hard-working people from the common stock. They sit together, eat together, argue about God together, indifferent to caste, birth or station. And all this is happening in the city of Kalyan - my Kalyan! (22)

Bijjala calls them insufferable moralists and narrates a verse of Basavanna.

Do not steal.

Do not kill.

Do not ever lie.

Do not rage... (21)

He knows that the sharanas are the real devotees and praises 'their bhakti, their incessant craving for the Lord's grace' (22). Bijjala understands the ground reality that Basavanna and his men are the real seekers of God and remarks:

I've built temples to keep my subjects happy. But the one truth I know is that I exist and God doesn't (22).

The play foregrounds the idea of the existence of God. Karnad retreats to the existentialist philosophy which focuses on the issue of presence or absence of God in the contemporary world. The idea here is that the king owes his existence to happiness of his subjects. He has built temples not for god but for his people. It is hard not to connect this twelfth century situation with the modern day philosophy of nihilism as well. Basavanna is not just a character in *Tale-Danda*. He is also a spokesperson for modernity, who believes that loving God's creatures means loving God. He rejects the empty rhetoric of the sycophants, who talk of immortalising the king through inscriptions and titles that will outlast the ages and will glorify the King for generations. He makes a significant comment:

Inscriptions need eyes to decipher them. Panegyrics need tongues to sing them. Meaning is generated by this moving body and it is this human body that should be our primary concern (25).

Basavanna also embodies the quality of fearlessness. In an argument, he dwells on the issue of leadership and tries to convey to Bijjala that the prince Somdeva in order to get the title of Yuvraj must undertake certain responsibilities. Karnad portrays him as a true well-wisher who always gives the right advice:

Kingship is a calling. A source of living, yes, but also a duty and a service to humanity. It is not an inheritance, not a family gift but a right to be earned, to be justified by diligent application.

His words carry great significance in the context of the contemporary political situations, when politicians of all hues want their children to be their successors. Bijjala argues that

'A son is the final goal of human existence, no matter how much he troubles you' (27). He feels that "it is a son who will keep your soul fed till eternity" (27). Basavanna refutes his argument tersely:

Physical parentage is of no consequence. A person is born truly only when the guru initiates him into a life of knowledge (27).

Basavanna believs that it is not just relationships that matter but the meanings one brings to them. He tells Bijjala that Sovideva hungers for his father's love, affection and attention. Basavanna, like all righteous characters of Karnad has to pay a price for speaking the truth. Sovideva tried to set a trap for Basavanna, who is sincere, well meaning and not a charlatan. Karnad's distaste for the modern godmen and their miracles is reflected in the following comment of Machanna, the king's advisor.

... since the winds of Bhakti started sweeping across the continent, the gods seem only too eager to act. The devotee weeps and God performs a miracle. The devotee laughs and He performs another. Our gods have been transformed into a mob of perpetual conjurers. (29)

Contrasted with these hypocritical imposters, Basavanna stands for ethics in religion. He is unmindful of what people say about him:

Let them damn me as a thief, condemn me as a miracle - monger. I don't care. But to be damned as a devotee in the presence of all the great devotees! Tale-Danda!

I don't have in me bhakti enough to equal a sixth of a mustard seed. I'm an ekke, a swallow-wort among mangoes. How can I shamelessly call myself a devotee in front of the sharanas of our Lord of the meeting of rivers?(30)

Through Basavanna and the portrayal of 'sharanas', Karnad emphasizes how institutionalized religion has created a class of idlers, who do not want to work. However, 'sharanas' are the people who firmly believe that work is worship and that work is not merely a profession but a calling. The city of Kalyan was benefitted by the trade and commerce that came pouring into the city along with the sharanas. This made the city prosperous. The king adds that the "sharanas seeks only to earn the day's keep, make no extra demands, treat profits with contempt" (31).

Karnad's hits out at meaningless rituals and dead and worn out conventions. When Jagadeva, a follower of Basavanna has to carry out ceremonial funeral rituals at his father's death, he clearly states that he had to perform this 'Brahmanical masquerade' (35) for the peace of mind of his mother. Karnad's works emphasize that rituals do not bring peace of mind. The similar idea is brought to the fore in the following words of Jagadeva about his father:

For all his fire sacrifices, penance and mediations, when it came to facing death, he couldn't take it. He was afraid. He used to weep with fear. Do you think my life too will be like that? A tale of fear, defeat, futility? (36)

As the frame story shifts to the central issue, that is, the alliance between a Brahmin girl and a cobbler's son, Karnad highlights another complex issue of modem existence, that is, the issue of inter-caste marriages. For some it is a cause for celebration. Basavanna, however, can foresee the impending storm. He says:

Until now it was only a matter of theoretical speculation. But this, this is real. The orthodox will see this mingling of castes as a blow at the very roots of the varnashrama dharma... I need hardly describe what venom will gush out, what hatred will erupt once the news spreads. (45)

There is a poignant portrayal in The Fire and The Rain *of the love story of Nittilai, a low caste girl and Aravasu a Brahmin. In* Tale-Danda *Karnad once again introduces a similar situation, this time between a cobbler's son and a Brahmin girl. Basavanna wistfully imagines the time when the curse of caste system will no longer breach the bond of love:*

Some day this entire edifice of caste and creed, this poison-house of varnashrama, will come tumbling down. Every human being will see himself only as a human being. As a bhakta. *As a* sharana. *That is inevitable. But we have a long way to go, you know the most terrible crimes have been justified in the name of* sanatoria *religion. (46)*

Haralayya, the cobbler is afraid when Madhuvarsa Kalavati's father says that he should not hesitate to sacrifice his 'daughter's life to forward the cause of our great movement' (46). Haralayya replies:

The word 'sacrifice' strikes terror in me. Too long have my people sacrificed our women to the greed of the upper castes, our sons to their cosmic theories of rebirth. No more sacrifices, please. (46)

Lalita, Kalavati's mother narrates an example of 'blind superstition' when she says that on every full moon night, Goddess Dyamanva of the Banyan Tree speaks, and on one such day when it was a full moon fair, she prophesied that, "Rivers of blood will flow if the marriage takes place, she said, human limbs will rot in the streets" (49).

The oppressed of society have always paid a heavy price, if ever they refused to conform to the ways of the upper castes. The cobbler's fears are genuine. Karnad movingly portrays the predicament of those living on the margin. Their fears are real. History is witness to bloody carnage as a fallout of any defiance of caste laws. King Bijjala exclaims, "The wedding pandal will turn into a slaughterhouse. The streets of Kalyan will reek of human entrails" (54).

The King seems worried as the resultant violence will lead to the collapse of trade and economy and the city will be in chaos. People of the city Kalyan have pledged to stop the 'unnatural alliance'. Therefore mercenaries and fighters are getting ready on the one hand and the houses of the sharanas turning into armouries on the other.

By referring to the contemporary issues in India, the roots exponents decolonized the Indian theatre in the real sense of the term bringing it close to the hearts of ordinary men and women. Karnad's drama often focuses on the philosophy of non-violence. He makes his characters articulate a distaste for violence. Therefore, in the violence-ridden times of today,

Karnad's plays acquire immense relevance .In Tale-Danda, his objective is to depict the innate violence of society, which is evident in the reaction of the so-called civilized people, who cannot bear to see change, even if it is for the better. Society has always reacted violently in the event of any challenge that enlightened minds pose to the existing socio-cultural norms. Bijjala orders the Sharanas not to go ahead with the wedding. The wedding, however, does take place amidst raging controversy. The priest defends the cast hierarchy and declares that "even those said to be its victims have embraced its logic of inequality" (63). Basavanna, has always opposed violence, even when his own people the Sharanas indulged in it: "Violence is wrong, whatever the provocation. To resort to it because someone else started it first is even worse. And to do so in the name of structure of brick and mortar is a monument to stupidity" (36) The king, having finally accepted the marriage between Brahmin girl and the cobbler's son, has incurred the wrath of people and is the first victim of violence. His own son imprisons him, letting on that the king had voluntarily retired. Subsequently, he is killed by Jagdeva, who eventually stabs himself.

The next victim of violence is Harallayya, whose son had married the Brahmin girl. The soldiers unleash cruelty of worst kind on the cobbler and his tribe:

It's harrowing! A while ago - the King's soldiers arrested Haralayya and took him to the city square... And then -then as the city watched - they plucked their eyes out -Plucked out their eyes with iron rods - bound them hand and foot and had them dragged through the streets - tied to elephants' legs -

Ayyo! How can I tell you? - Torn limbs along the lanes, torn entrails, flesh, bones - They died screaming! (90)

His wife ran down the streets, screaming towards a lake or a well. The city of Kalyan dropped dead with deserted streets like a cemetery. Basavanna, having seen all the dying people cries out in pain:

Whose name? And whose face? Whose wound and whose blood? This carcass is mine. Am I also the King's slayer. So this is the last of Allama's tableaux. The festivities are over, the streets deserted. The night has departed and the world is silent. (99)

The Lord of the Meeting Rivers is once again called upon by Basavanna to absorb the darkness until light enters again.. Basavanna envisions an era of self-realisation, of happiness within, where everything will be enlightened by light. "Light within light. The great dawn of light" (99). He invokes the Lord for illuminating light which would wash away the darkness, and enlighten the thoughts and mind of people.

But before the light enters there is unrelenting darkness and dance of death on the streets of Kalyan. There is anarchy all over. People rushing through the streets, howling and screaming. Temples were sacked and the city is abuzz with gruesome tales of rape, murder and rioting. A messenger informs that Basavanna is no more, he merged with the elements. The sharanas flee Kalyan and scatter in all eight directions. Sovideva orders his soldiers to pursue them and not let them escape.

Men, women, children - cut them all down. Set the hounds after them. Search each wood, each bush. Burn the houses that give them shelter. Burn their books. Yes, the books! Tear them into shreds and consign them to the wells. Their voices shall be stilled for ever - (101)

It is not only the wild and violent impulses of the ruler and the people that the play highlights, but also the fact that regressive attitudes spell an inherent violence. The new and revolutionary ideas always meet with resistance. Sovideva calls the 'sharanas', "the villains! The traitors!", Who killed his father. In a long speech he dwells on the importance of a King to his people. His hypocrisy is all too evident here. He had put his father behind bars and now offers the following advice to his subjects:

The King is father to his people and the people shall love him and obey him like his offspring. No tongue shall wag against the King or his family or his retinue or his officers... For the King is God incarnate! (101)

He also orders that all sharanas, foreigners, and free thinkers be expelled from the city of Kalyan. Women and the lower orders should live within the norms prescribed by the ancient tradition otherwise they will suffer like dogs. Every citizen must consider himself a soldier always ready to lay down his life for the King.

Fire erupts in the background and the sky is filled with screams. Vedic chants are sung. The eulogies begin and drown everything else. Sovideva is crowned as the king, who "continues to gesticulate violently" (102). The fire in the background continues to blaze.

The note on which Kamad concludes the play is a significant one. On the one hand a new era of light has dawned with light of enlightenment. It is clear that the light of knowledge spread by Basavanna will stay forever even after his death. On the other hand, the reins of power are taken over by Sovideva who could never earn the respect of the people of Kalyan. The dualism persists as ever, since ages. The co-existence of power and corruption is once against reflected upon. Aparna Dharwadker aptly remarks that "to understand the present one must return to the past, because the pre-modern history of India prefigures and encompasses the drama of modernity" (Karnad, Vol. 2, X), as the play is replete with instances of caste discrimination which can be related to the twelfth-century history of the 'sharnas' as well as to present-day cultural politics in India. In a country like India, 'caste is ultimately transcendable' (Dharwadker, Vol. 2, xii) and "the effects of intra-religious conflict are very similar to those of inter-religious conflict" (Dharwadker, Vol. 2, xiii).

Tale Danda, thus, carries many significant references to the turmoil of the modern India. Girish Karnad skilfully draws a parallel between a twelfth century scenario and the present day conflicts. In this play he not only underscores the issues of caste discrimination and violence perpetrated on the marginalized of society, but also highlights the resistance that is always encountered by those who dare to challenge the traditions.

The Dreams of Tipu Sultan : Creating a post Colonial Context

Karnad's play *The Dreams of Tipu Sultan* deals with one of the most important historical figures of the Indian history, Tipu Sultan. The play was commissioned by the BBC to celebrate the fiftieth anniversary of India's independence and it was broadcast as a radio play in London on the 15th August, 1997. It depicts the life and vision of Tipu Sultan (the then King of Mysore) in the last phase of his life. Karnad has very adeptly handled the task of presenting before us a lively picture of the Tiger of Mysore, whom the British destroyed for his legendary tiger-like spirit. Ironically, the invitation came to Karnad from the land of the erstwhile rulers. As noted earlier, the British Broadcasting Corporation commissioned the play. Aparna Dharwadkar points out:

Karnad confronts British colonialism in its crucial early stages of military expansion - paradoxically, at the invitation of the British, and for a celebration of Indian independence (Dharwadker, Vol. 2, xxii).

The play is extremely significant in the context of postcolonialism as it takes into account the early attempts of the colonizers to establish their supremacy in India. Since the concept of the 'nation' was still far-fetched, the British spared no efforts to pit the Indian rulers against each other, who had their individual spheres of power.

Like the other history plays of Karnad, the context is authentically Indian in *Tipu Sultan.* Karnad acknowledges that he owes his obsession with Tipu also to A.K. Ramanujan, who spoke to him of Tipu's secret diary. Karnad also strongly felt that Tipu needed to be given his due as one of the most important figures in the early years of British colonialism. As a result Karnad's play evinces "the impulse towards a complex poetic rehabilitation of Tipu" (Dharwadkar, xxiii). Dharwadkar further observes:

In many important respects Tipu Sultan *follows the model of the history play established in* Tughlaq *and* Tale- Danda. *It draws upon a range of historical sources to present convincing portraits of the principal characters, but creates an imaginative plot and resonant dialogue to contain their experience. It deals with a controversial protagonist who can be characterized in radically opposite ways, depending on the observer's viewpoint—as a heroic figure of anticolonial resistance (comparable to the Rani of Jhansi) in one perspective, and a treacherous but fallible (and even foolish) adversary in another. (Dharwadker, Vol. 2, xxiii)*

Tipu Sultan was, perhaps, among the very few, who offered resistance to the British. He was also, perhaps, the only one who tried his best to convince the native rulers about the cunning of the English. In refusing to bow down before them, he gave evidence of his courage. A true martyr in the annals of Indian history, he was forgotten, while the rulers, who sided with the British continued to reap benefits of privy-purses even after the British were gone. In Karnad's play, which is set in 1803, the events of Tipu's life and times are unfolded in flashback.

Perhaps, one of the most important issues Karnad takes up in the play is about the way history has been written, distorted and re-presented by the oriental scholars. In the name of objective portrayal of events, the British historians often provided highly subjective accounts of historical occurrences. When the play opens, the scene is set in front of the big mosque in Seringapatam, in the year 1803 in the city of Mysore, where historian Mir Hussain Ali Khan Kirmani talks with colonel Colin Mackenzie, the oriental scholar. Mackenzie asks Kirmani "to develop a certain objectivity" and "to keep emotions out and stick to the facts" in order to write history of Tipu Sultan, in particular about his last days. The character of Hussain Ali Kirmani "enables Karnad to reflect on the process of history-writing and the many conduits of history - oral and written, unofficial and official, objective and subjective, dominant and subaltern" (Dharwadker, Vol. 2, xxiv).

Kirmani refers to Tipu's last dreams that were recorded in his diary. In a flashback Kirmani reminisces about Sultan's last day when he was staying in the 'Caravanserai' on the northern ramparts:

The English had launched their assault... He buckled on his sword beer, took out an envelope from his pocket, sealed it and gave it to me: 'Keep it till I come back', he said... He mumbled a prayer and left. I'll never forget that expression on his face. (Karnad, Two Plays, 9)

The next day when Kirmani broke open the seal, inside was a paper on which Sultan had recorded the dream he had had the previous night: "His last dream, with that my history ends. Yours begins. (Pause)" (9)

Karnad's play foregrounds the way the Oriental scholars wrote history to justify the British rule. Their attitude was at best one of derision and contempt. The play moves between different chronological sequences. As events are unfolded by Colonel Mackenzie, his subjective intent is more than evident. He had spotted,Sultan's body on the night of the 4th of May, under a pile of corpses. Eventually the body "Corpulent, with big twirly moustaches, round face..." is recognized by Wellesley. And then follows the conversation between Mackenzie and Wellesley, cold, matter of fact and insensitive:

So that's the Tiger of Mysore...

"Is he alive?" Mackenzie : Is he?

Wellesley: He is warm, but that wound on his temple couldn't have survived that.

(A chorus of voices, mainly female is heard wailing in the far distance. They listen.)

Wellesley: If we were looking for confirmation, I suppose that's it.

(The wailing gets louder and spreads. The entire city is soon wailing). (14)

The play further highlights the way little regard was shown by the whites even for men of Tipu Sultan's status. The callous disregard with which the soldier who had promised his friend a present, chops off Tipu's moustache, which is lightly dismissed by Mackenzie as 'an act of vandalism' is among many instances of the colonizers humiliating the natives and the historian's attempts to dismiss these as instances as trivial. Kirmani further highlights the atrocities of the British soldiers at Tipu Sultan lay dead: "Every house looted. Every available woman raped. Soldiers throwing away precious jewellery because they could not carry any more."(16)

The play underscores the insensitivity of the oriental historians, who sometimes forced even the Indian scholars to give completely fabricated and damaging accounts of the Indian rulers and more so of the self-respecting figures like Tipu Sultan. Kirmani, who was close to Tipu is unable to document history as desired by the white masters. He feels that his wounds are still fresh, even though "the blood and tears dried up a long time ago". He admits there has been no healing. Mackenzie insists that Kirmani must write about Tipu's embassy to Mauritius—the Malarctic adventure, to which Kirmani says that it never took place. Mackenzie, however, insists that Lord Mornington had absolute proof of Tipu's mischief. At this Kirmani snaps, giving enough evidence of his moral courage: "Perhaps His Lordship was dreaming ... But dreaming is not dishonourable. My Master, Tipu Sultan dreamt. (16)"

In other respects, Tipu Sultan *stands apart in Karnad's oeuvre because as a play about colonialism it has to grapple with the inescapable psychodrama of East vs. West, Europe vs. The non-European other, white vs. Non-white, and colonizer vs. Colonized. Avoiding any partisan parade of heroes and villains, Karnad creates ambitious and determined players in both camps who are sucked into the vortex of a major transitional moment in Indian history, politics, and culture. (Dharwadker, Vol.2, xxiv)*

It is revealed that Tipu was in a habit of keeping a record of his dreams and on the night when Tipu was buried there was a thunderstorm and everything was destroyed in which Kirmani lost those precious papers. In Kirmani's words, the storm: "... wiped away every word written in ink, within a night, all my recorded facts became memory" (17). The play forges a connection between history and memory—a connection that underlies histories of all great men:

There are several important strategies in the portrayal of Tipu Sultan that unfold simultaneously. Karnad interlineates 'textualised' history and legend, lore, and memory because all these of modes of transmission are germane to the story of Tipu. The ruler's fabled persona as the Tiger of Mysore thus figures prominently in the action, both as oral legend and as a military reality that the English must contend with. (Dharwadker, Vol.2, xxiv)

Tipu's diary was kept concealed from his closest confidants. Suddenly Tipu's voice is heard to which only Kirmani reacts. Tipu's voice: "In this register are recorded the dreams I've had and am having (17)" Kirmani also emphasizes that Sultan had hidden the diary under his pillow and there it had lain after his death... It was sacred, personal. Mackenzie on the other hand is dismissive as usual: "I'm afraid we merely saw it as an old little book. A pleasantly inconsequential conversation piece (Ironic)"(17).

Kirmani being very thoughtful is somewhat bewildered. He tells Mackenzie that there were blank pages in Tipu's diary and wondered what dreams he meant to record there, and what he did not, will never be known. Many aspects of Tipu's personality are unfolded through his dreams. He comes across

...as a beloved ruler, legendary warrior, loving father, and visionary dreamer, but also as the Machiavellian schemer who plots with the French against the English, the defeated soldier who enters into humiliating treaties with the enemy, and the gullible commander who is eventually betrayed by his own side. (Dharwadker, Vol. 2, xxiv)

Kirmani and Mackenzie now act as choric characters commenting on the action. Kirmani narrates the following dream of Tipu. As dreams are narrated one after the other, many aspects of Tipu's personality are unfolded. He comes across as an ambitious statesman, cherishing dreams of making his kingdom prosperous, modern and ideal:

...I was returning with my army from Farrukhi near Salamabad when I had the following dreams... I had been on an elephant Shikar with Poornaiya, the Finance Minister, when we saw a big temple. It was in a dilapidated state, and I said: 'Poornaiya, look at that structure. It looks quite mysterious. (18)

They see a strange building with several human images. The images are not of gods and as they move their eyes, two women stand-up draped in nine-yard saris. They inform Tipu that the two of them are living women seeking their salvation. Tipu feels sorry if he had disturbed them and offers them help. Tipu asks Poornaiya to get the temple repaired so that the seekers of God may not be disturbed. As they walk out of the temple they see two old men who inform them that they are the envoys of the Emperor of China who has sent a white elephant and the horses as a token of friendship and affection. The old men also tells him that the Emperor had never sent these gifts to anyone except him and the Great Alexander with the intention of providing the practical knowledge. Tipu then interprets his dream and says that: "... God Almighty and our Prophet will make me another Alexander..."(21).

In another scene Tipu moves to the Diwan-i-Khas along with Mir Sadiq and Poornaiya where he holds a conference. He expresses his desire to send a delegation to France. Through Monsieur Piere Monneron he has. arranged a meeting with the French Governor General of Mauritius. The Governor General has agreed to talk to the King of France and arrange an audience. Tipu asks Osman Khan to lead the delegation but admits he is envious of him:"Actually, how I wish I could go with you. I envy you!" Osman Khan adding to this says that 'the King of France would have been happier to deal with a quicker intelligence'. In the list drawn up for delegation, he asks to add silkworms and eggs from the island of Iezeriah Diraz near Muscat, which may suit. Tipu also expresses his desire to bring glass, guns and cannons.

For centuries we begged and borrowed silk from the Chinese. And everyone predicted disaster when I got a few eggs from

China. And now we have a flourishing industry of our own. (22)

Tipu then asks Osman Khan that he will give a letter for King Louis, so as to explain the situation in India. Tipu expresses his desire that King Louis can sign a treaty with the French, a treaty of Perpetual Alliance, so that he can order the French soldiers to march under him, then he could change the face of India. He asks Ghulam Ali Khan to bring with them "not just the ten thousand soldiers, but French craftsman who could make guns, cannons, pistols" (24). A brave king, Tipu not only never bowed down to the British and French rulers, but also wanted an equal relationship with them. The economic interests of the country were always paramount to him.

Karnad also gives us a glimpse of India when countries like Turkey, Arabia, Iran were clamouring for the products available in India. "The Imam of Muscat has fallen in love with the sandalwood and spices of India" (24) and they also permitted to build a factory for such products in Muscat, thereby providing good opportunities for business at both ends. Tipu is thoughtful about trade, industry and money. Karnad here gives us a glimpse of economic development at that period of time in the history, of India from where India marched on and ensured a place for herself in foreign market.

Tipu Sultan, in Karnad's play is a real visionary. He is like any modem statesman, who is open to look up to any nation of the world for technical and economic cooperation. Not only the doctors, surgeons, blacksmiths, locksmiths and cutters will come to India to introduce the latest in these traders, but also the gardener who would go to work at Lai Bagh and produce new varieties of trees, flowers and bushes.

We need new ideas... Europe - it's full of new ideas - inventions - all kinds of machines - bursting with energy(25).

A truly modern minded king, he explains to Ghulam Ali what a thermometer is. Tipu explains it as a quicksilver in a glass tube and when placed in the hands of a sick man the silver rises to a certain degree and indicates the height of his disorder, which helps the hakim to decide on the treatment. Poornaiya expresses his disbelief on hearing this and says that he looks forward to see this instrument. Akbar Khan remarks that "This is like a dream come true, your Majesty", Tipu asks them to prepare for their journey and to spend good times with their families as they will not see them for a couple of years. The children, Fath Haider and Murzuddin, consider it a marvellous idea and expresses their desire to join the delegation but Tipu turns down their request on the ground saying that they have to prepare for a different world.

Poomaiya then informs Tipu that the English and the French have signed a treaty in Versailles according to which neither is allowed to enter into the local affairs in India. Tipu in a thoughtful mood says that the French and the English are neighbours - they cannot be friends forever. They are bound to start quarrelling. Tipu here makes a reference to the new Governor General Lord Cornwallis who is a defeated General and who lost the war in America to a farmer caller Washington. Tipu adds that: "... to get the stain off his reputation, he needs to vanquish one man in India - only one - Tipu Sultan!"(28).

Tipu turns to the audience, as the stage darkens. There is an abrupt shift in scene and he narrates his dream once again.

On the sixth day of the... I was preparing for a night attack on the Maratha armies... I had a dream. (28)

Tipu in his dream saw a young man, turbaned like a Maratha, who turns out to be a woman. Tipu interprets the dream once again and associates it with the Marathas who are dressed in male attire but in truth are women.

The scene again changes abruptly to the Maratha court in Pune where Nana Phadnavis, the Maratha statesman is present along with Charles Malet - who is the representative of Lord Cornwallis, who conspires and provokes the Marathas to declare war on Tipu. Malet says that the Governor General hopes that the Maratha chief will use this opportunity and recover the territories seized unjustly by Tipu Sultan's father Haider Ali and ... will join us "in punishing a man who we believe is the enemy of all mankind"(33).

Karnad acquaints us with India of the eighteenth century when the land was rich and overflowing with goods the world thirsted for. But Indian princes were "... comatose wrapped in their opium dreams", who, thought Tipu, would wake up one day and throw out the Europeans. Tipu also adds that: "The Marathas of Pune are coy, flirtatious, unreliable. But I need their help, so I've made peace with them" (36).

At this moment Hasina enters and informs that the vakils have returned from Pune and the Marathas have declared war on them. Hearing this Ruquayya gasps and cannot breathe, a Hakim is called upon to see her. Mackenzie then informs us that Lord Cornwallis invaded Mysore in 1790, with the parallel attacks of the Nizam and the Marathas. The war stretched for two long years. When Cornwallis reached the foot of the fort of Seringapatam and saw the futility of trying to capture it, he retreated disheartened. He wrote to his friend that his spirits are worn out and if he cannot soon overcome Tipu "the plagues and mortifications of this most difficult war will overcome me" (37). Kirmani tells us that the English forces ran into the Marathas with their abundant supplies, the two then joined forces and attacked Seringapatam. Tipu Sultan was forced to sue for peace.

Karnad's argument in the play is that the English were successful in India not because they were militarily superior but mainly because of their policy of divide and rule. Since the concept of nation had still not come into being so there was a decentring of power relations. Tipu seems to embody the strength of a

...proto-nationalist who resists as long as he can the Englishman's schemes to rob his land, even as he understands that the English 'believe in the destiny of their race' and are willing to die in faraway places for their dream of England. At home, however, his appeals to a common faith fail to rally the Muslim Nizam to his side, and the instinctive hostility between Hindu and Muslim princes alienates him from the Marathas, although he issues a prophetic (and purely political) warning to the Nana about England's territorial ambitions. (Dharwadker, Vol. 2, xxv)

However, he is not able to bring the Hindu and Muslim Kings to a rallying point. In spite of his issuing a warning to Nana Phadnavis about the ambitious and dark designs of the British, he does not succeed in persuading these local Kings to stand united against the British. To quote Dharwadker again:

The pained scenes of Tipu's peace treaties with the English emphasize that a complex, civilized, and prosperous culture was betrayed into subjection because of the pursuit of petty self-interest by key functionaries. In hindsight, the 'traitorous' collaboration between English and native armies across racial and cultural lines... the perfect prelude and antithesis to the invention of India – as - the nature of nineteenth and twentieth-century nationalists, (xxvi)

Karnad's play carries the overtones of the love hate relationship, that is, 'ambivalence' which Homi Bhaba describes as a combination of repulsion and a attraction between the colonizers and the colonized. The British, suggests the play, find Tipu Sultan invincible. When the terms of treaty are read out by Poornaiya at Tipu's insistence, the apparent fear of Tipu in the mind of British becomes clear. The first out of the four terms - was that all the English prisoners taken by Tipu and his father be released unconditionally, secondly, cession of half the domain; third, an indemnity of six crores and the last which Poornaiya hesitates to read out.

... two hostages, the two sons of the Sultan", to be handed over to the English as hostages of war, until the terms of the treaty are agreed upon, signed and sealed. (41)

An uproar of angry protests is heard from the crowd, some call it 'outrageous' and some term it as 'barbaric'. The citizens request Tipu not to sue for peace on such humiliating terms. But the tiger of Mysore shows his spirit and with a heavy heart decides to send Abdul Khaliq, who is eight and Mirzuddin, only a few months younger, as war hostages. There is a reaction of horror, anger and revulsion among the crowd with the shouts of "No, please don't accept...", but Tipu has given his words now. His people warn Tipu about the danger involved in it but Tipu assures them that: "The English will not harm our children. They'll not poison them or kill them, for there's no financial profit in it... They'll not harm my children. (41)". But Tipu fears that they will teach his children a new language:

This is the new language that has come into land: English. This is the culture of that language: English. Boys of seven and eight as hostages of war. (42)

The danger is: they'll teach my children their language, English. The language in which it is possible to think of children as hostages. All I can try to do is agree to their terms and conclude the treaty in a hurry - before my children have learnt that language. (43)

Rather than accepting the destruction of his city, Tipu accepts the terms of the treaty. The meeting adjourns with this and the crowd departs in tears. On being asked by Poornaiya as to how will the Queen take the news of her sons to be sent as hostages, Tipu informs the nobleman:

God has been angry with us, Poornaiya. But He has not let us down entirely. I was late for this meeting because - I had to bid goodbye to Begum Ruquayya Banu. She left us this morning. (43)

Tipu with distress adds that "She died without knowing I had bartered her sons for my kingdom." He had ordered that there will be no wailing or weeping till his meeting was over. Wailing is then heard in the background. The grieved heartbroken Tipu expresses his sorrow in the following soliloquy:

The dead are happy. They go. And I've seen too many dead to care about death anymore. It's my sons I have to worry about now... (44)

Tipu has been portrayed by Karnad as being far ahead of his times. Language perhaps, was amongst the most powerful tools of the colonizers, which they used for subjugating the natives on the pretext of civilizing them. The postcolonial theory, amongst many other ways used by the colonizers to suppress the natives, refers to 'assimilation' through which aims to 'westernize' the colonized " to the extent of annihilating their identity. Tipu's fears, therefore, are real. He sends his sons with ceremonial splendour.

... as heroes, symbols of the glory of their land. In full splendour. A splendour that'll put the foreigners to shame -and cover up my own sense of shame. (44)

Lord Cornwallis receives them with his officers. The princes impress everyone:

... the dignity of their bearing and their self-possession drew praise, from every Englishman (48).

It is at this point in the play that Karnad addresses important issues such as colonialism, race and nation. As an atonement for his 'sin', Tipu decides to sleep on the bare stone floor till his sons are in foreign land. Reciting Sufi Zak's incantation, he suddenly sways in a trance and hears his father Haider's voice, who reprimands Tipu for offering his children to the enemy and also for letting Cornwallis go intentionally by not attacking him. Tipu is anguished and penitent as he vents out his feelings:

... I see myself in them - I see these white skins swarming all over the land and I wonder what makes them so relentless? Desperate? ... They don't give up. Nor would I. Sometimes I feel more confident of them than my own people. What makes them so unsparing towards themselves? Is it only money? No, if it was only for money, they would betray each other... They believe in the destiny of their race. Why can't we? (56)

Karnad portrays the main English characters in the play as heartless, calculating and ruthless, but self-assured. In a lengthy monologue Tipu voices the turmoil within him, referring to the inherent self assuredness of their race. He also knows the ugly truth that many of "his trusted officers" were secretly negotiating with Lord Cornwallis, but he couldn't expose them. He considered them as the pillars of his Kingdom, but they stabbed him in his back. Tipu at this point makes a significant remark that the English fight for something called England. In other words, they had a nation

- an entity that was missing in India at that point of time, as there were so many rulers, who were at loggerheads:

What is it? It's not a religion that sustains them, nor a land that feeds them... It's just a dream, for which they are willing to kill and die. Children of England! They have conquered our land, plundered its riches. And now they've started taking away our children. Mine -. (52)

This idea is further strengthened as the scene shifts to the Maratha camp where Tipu Sultan meets Hari Pant Phadke and makes him realise the treachery of the Marathas and warns him against the English who will take his children next time. Tipu makes him realise his mistake and says:

You are back where you were while the English now have the entire coastline of India. And remember, they are a seafaring power. Mine is a landlocked kingdom, so I thirst for the sea, for today the sea is the key to power, to prosperity.(54)

Mackenzie and Kirmani comment on the defeat of Tipu and the personal triumph for Lord Cornwallis who got the title of 'Marquis'. After two years, Tipu's sons were restored. Richard Wellesley, Second Earl of Mornington comes to take over the charge. The scene takes place in 1798 in Calcutta where Richard Wellesley and Colonel William Kirkpatrick and Arthur Wellesley, younger brother of Richard Wellesley are present. Mornington makes it clear that "the Board of Control has made it clear that the East India Company was not to acquire any more territory in India" (55). He could not see Tipu growing in "power and prestige", and adds that "longer the peace, the strong will

Tipu become". The scene once again shifts to Diwan-i-Aam. Mir Sadiq, Poornaiya, Qamaruddin and Nadeem Khan are informed by Tipu about the new demands of the English—four of Tipu's sons as war hostages and half of his Kingdom. Tipu further adds that:

Today I am the only one in India who won't bow and scrape before them. So they want to humiliate me. I'm told England is buzzing with stories of what a monster I am and how I need to be subdued. (60)

The play foregrounds Tipu as a great and courageous ruler, who causes discomfiture to the British because of his toughness. His noblemen assure Tipu that they will fight "the English to the bitter end... to the last drop of our blood." The seer of the Monastery at Sringeri conveys his support to him. Fath Haider informs his father about the forces ready to attack the enemy. Poornaiya makes Tipu sure that victory will be theirs, as the stars, according to the Chief Astrolonger of the Ranganatha Temple, are propitious: "The nine planets have been placated and offerings made to the guardians of the eight directions (62)" . Mir Sadiq comes with the news that the Nizam has realised his folly in backing the English and the Marathas have made up their mind to support the Sultan. Qamaruddin depicts the scene where the English are seen withdrawing.

Tipu is congratulated, Fath Haider asks Tipu to attack the English. Tipu tells him that they will celebrate today with prayers to God. Poornaiya owes all this to the vision of the future which Tipu has given to them. Abdul Khaliq, at this moment informs Tipu that Mother says the rose bush has blossomed and he must come to see it. Tipu then invites all the Zenanas to the ramparts "to see the white plague depart. Let's all watch a new era drawn" (64).

This was Tipu's last dream. That afternoon he was killed in the battle. Roar of tigers is heard in the background followed by gunfire and then silence prevails. As the Sultan is killed, his tigers in the palace are shot dead, while the mechanical tiger was shipped off to London. Kirmani makes a remark that: "It was not Tipu's dreams but his predictions that came true" (65).

Karnad mentions in the end as postscript that when India became independent in 1947, the families of maharajas who bowed before the British masters were granted sumptuous privy purses by the Government of India while the descendants of Tipu Sultan were left to rot in the slums of Calcutta. This, perhaps, is one of the greatest ironies of independent India, that the accolades seldom go to the ones who deserve them.

Tipu falls to the bullets but not from grace till the end unlike other princes. In his fall he emerges as the real tiger of Mysore, who could cause terror to the British, even as he lay dead. Karnad has skilfully blended the character of Tipu as a father figure and Tipu as the tiger of Mysore. His public persona and his personal traits are well highlighted as his inner self is revealed before us scene by scene through his dreams. He is vindicated in his death as a symbol of India's pride, India's real Tiger who continues to be one of the most inspiring figures in the history of India.

Karnad presents Tipu as the seeker for peace and prosperity. He made every possible attempt to convince the Marathas and the Nizam about the game of power politics of the English, who followed the policy of 'divide and rule' in ruining India.

The play has a well developed and compact plot and the action reveals the way colonialism spread its tentacles in India. Tipu could foresee the trap of colonisation and warned the Marathas and the Nizams in spite of the fact they did not support him. He died for his people and died as a martyr than as a victim. Grace Sudhir aptly remarks that:

Both as a soldier and King, he fought fearlessly like a tiger, never crouching but couchant - stalking and facing the enemy head on. (Grace, 308-17)

At the very outset, Karnad advises to resists the temptation for using masks, special lighting or costume for the dream scenes. He also adds that it is essential for the total impact of the play that the dreams are staged realistically.

The historical references like the Malarctic deal and Pitt's India Act, takes us back to the point of time in the history of India's independence when the meaning of independence was actually valued. Like other plays, where Karnad uses historical figures, this play too has immense contemporary value as it provokes us to make a fresh assessment of how valuable freedom is in the present day context.

Conclusion

Girish Karnad has enriched the contemporary Indian theatre with his ingenuity and powerful plays. Being one of the foremost exponents of the 'theatre of roots' movement, he pioneered a style which presents an amalgam of traditional Indian theatre and modern sensibility. Karnad's plays exhibit the inherent characteristics of the roots movements, which is modern theatre with a typical Indian flavour. As pointed out earlier, the term 'theatre of roots' was coined by Dr. Suresh Awasthi in the year 1918 to recapitulate modern Indian theatre's struggle to liberate itself from western realistic theatre. The roots movement was conceptualized by the playwrights to restore India's cultural identity and to challenge the colonial aesthetics. An analysis of Karnad's plays bears out that he has contributed greatly towards the 'decolonization' of Indian theatre. Along with other exponents of the roots movement, he is credited with imparting a distinctly Indian touch to the contemporary theatre as well as liberating it from the monotony of the purely western dramatic idiom. To achieve this, Karnad takes recourse to the classical Indian dramaturgy, folk theatre traditions and historical legends.

Karnad's plays are consciously anchored in the ancient theory and tradition of Indian theatre. They reflect the technical ingenuity of the traditional Indian theatrical art, while he innovates and experiments by upholding contemporary views. He demystifies the dominant beliefs and practices of traditional Indian theatre. The myths are incorporated as plots. However, he does not present them in their original form. He seems to question their validity and puts them on trial. In his efforts to re-conceptualize the mythic tales, he never loses sight of the modern sensibility. The human obsession for immortality is well exhibited in *Yayati*. *Yayati* illustrates the influence of the *Yakṣhagana* performances that Karnad had seen during his formative years in Sirsi in rural Karnataka. The play mirrors his inner conflicts as well. Pooru's dilemma has been handled by Karnad in an existential vein. In Chitralehka's character, one can find the note of self-assertion, that in intrinsically modern. As a Rhodes scholar Karnad wanted to explore his potentials as a playwright and he ended up writing a play which reflected on the 'emotional intimidation of the young by the old' (Balaram, 1) through the story of king Yayati. The myth of Yayati also brings to the fore the conflict between tradition and modernity. *The Fire and the Rain* also underscores issues such as parricide, fratricide, caste and class disparities. Karnad uses the techniques of traditional Sanskrit drama by bringing in 'yajna' and the motif of fire sacrifice. These techniques he blends with the western practice of inviting audience participation through introducing the Actor-manager, who comments on the play that is enacted by the characters of *The Fire and the Rain* . *Bali : The Sacrifice* deals with the obnoxious practice of animal sacrifice and resurgence of protest against it. In the modern violence ridden times, the play offers a tribute to the theme of non-violence. As such his theatre brings forth the timeless significance of mythological stories. The traditional narratives thus acquire an aura that grips the sensibility of modern theatre-goers.

Being part of the "formative generation" of Indian playwrights who "collectively reshaped Indian theatre as a major national institution in the later twentieth century." (Dharwadker, Vol. 2, vii) , Karnad emerges as a major trend- setter in the contemporary history of drama in India. He "re-articulates what it means to be Indian in India" (Mee, 288). The dramaturgical structures and aesthetical aspects of Indian regional theatre are put to use by Karnad "to redirect the modern Indian theatre" (Mee, 96). From the mythological renderings of *Ramayana* and the *Mahabharata*, to the interreligious and intra-religious issues, Karnad's works culminate in re-presenting the Indian culture in the contemporary context, as aspired by the roots practitioners.

Karnad through his works 'decolonized' Indian theatre by challenging the colonial construction of theatre "as a text-based phenomenon by (re) turning to 'indigenous' performance-driven theatre" (Mee, 95). Having a close connection with the traditional 'folk' forms of Indian theatre like Ramlila, Rasleela, Yakshagana, Jatra and Svang, the roots movement revived the cultural folk forms of story-telling and folk theatre to resist the colonial culture.

Based on his serious explorations of folklore, the subjects of his plays reflect the problems and challenges of contemporary life and endeavour to forge a link between the past and the present, thereby re-defining the Indian folk-theatre. Karnad refers to the influence of the folk-theatre as an important aspect the blossoming of his creative faculties. Since he was aware of the power of this drama he s

"....theatre forms borrowed from the west [were] totally inadequate for effectively projecting the social aspirations, way of life, cultural patterns and fundamental problems of contemporary India (Mee, 7).

He therefore, reverted to the ancient Hindu mythology and legends to represent the past making it relevant to contemporary India. Karnad's drama is all about re-presenting the known and the familiar in a novel manner. By using folk-tales, mythological and historical legends, he "weaves together timeless truths about human life and emotions contained in ancient Indian epics, legends and Upanishads" (Gupta, 249). A remarkable feature of Karnad's works is the use of rich variety of themes which create an innovative style. In most of his plays he experiments boldly with the myths and legends from the epics *Ramayana* and the *Mahabharata*, making them relevant to the modern times. One finds in his writings a basic simplicity and naturalness coupled with a meaningful depth.

His plays deal with a broad range of subjects, and are imbued with a socio-historical perspective. He foregrounds the social context of individual conflict by examining various social issues. Karnad voices the issue of communal tension in his play *Taledanda*. The play takes up the issue of the reformist movement, Virshaivism and displays the descent of a civil and cultured society into anarchy and terror

Another notable feature of Karnad's theatre is that he extends the practices of the theatre of roots movement by combining traditional genres and western technicalities to evolve a new theatrical idiom known as the hybrid theatre. The technique of fringing together myths, legends and folk narrative is his forte. His plays are enriched with all these elements. He takes recourse to ancient texts like *Kathasaritasagar* and thirteenth century Kannada epic *Yashodhara* Charite, to structure his plays. The idea of human perfection rooted in the ancient Indian texts is well exploited by Karnad in his play *Hayavadana*. The play also constitutes the universal theme of unifying the mind and body to achieve perfection. Karnad also depicts the absurdist's notion of the futility of human existence in his plays. The existentialist crisis of modern man is conveyed through strong characters who are torn by intense psychological and philosophical battles raging within their mind. This aspect is dealt with in plays like *Hayavadana, Yayati, Naga-Mandala,* and *Bali:The Sacrifice.*

In *Hayavadana*, lord Ganesha who "is the god of threshold, of crossings over and, therefore, of transformations" (Mee, 158-9), is placed in the context of a Hindu ritual performance including Yakshagana. Karnad compels his audience to perceive what is termed as 'multi vocality'. Lord Ganesha becomes the embodiment of 'complex seeing', a technique practised by Bertolt Brecht.

In affinity with the Brechtian theatre, Karnad's theatre is a theatre with a purpose. He aims to shatter the 'illusion' of the theatre by which the spectators become so involved in a play that they forget, who they really are. Therefore, like Bertolt Brecht, Karnad works for the 'alienation effect' leaving the stage devices visible, making announcements and allowing the narrators directly talk to the audience. A fine example of this is *Hayavadana*, where Bhagavata speaks to the audiences in the course of the play and keeps them updating about the happenings, while reviewing each and every situation in the play. This is one of the finest examples where the Western technique mingles with an altogether traditional cultural practice to create a hybrid theatre. Similarly, *Naga-Mandala* , which combines the folk theatre with the western dramaturgy, is also an example of the hybrid theatre.

Karnad criticizes the social practices, beliefs and superstitions prevalent in India. He satirizes meaningless religious practices and beliefs. Karnad is also critical of social evils like 'sati'. He wants his audience to actually see and grasp the essence or the 'Satva' out of a performance which is the sole aim of theatre. The character of Padmini in *Hayavadana* emerges as a new woman who refuses to comply with the traditional image of an 'ideal' woman. *Naga Mandala* on the other hand presents a tale within a tale which urges the audience to look at societal mores in a new light. Karnad also uses the traditional device of shape-shifting as "a method of exploring differences and similarities between characters, situations, and ideas" (Paranjape, 95). Shape shifting is a common feature of the traditional and folk theatre. The metaphor of shape-shifting is found in folk tales, fairy tales and fables. In Karnad's plays shape-shifting is redolent with destruction and tragic death of the protagonists in the end. In *Naga Mandala* the Naga has to die when he assumes an altogether different shape.

Karnad experiments with a new genre in his monologue *Flowers*. Based on a folk-tale from Karnataka the monologue marks an important shift in Karnad's dramaturgy. Karnad recasts the legend and presents a conflict between the priests religious fervour (of decorating the lingam) and his erotic love for the courtesan. In theme and technique the monologue demarcates Karnad's career as a playwright. He highlights the spiritual and the aesthetic aspects of the story by presenting 'a pattern of triangulated desire' (Dharwadker, xxxii) between the priest, his wife and the courtesan. Karnad explores new dimensions and possibilities of the ancient aesthetic theory making it relevant to the modern times. In the modern context the monologue marks the advent of the eternal conflict between the body and soul.

The roots playwrights decolonized the theatre by incorporating historical events that made a great impact on Indian sensibility. The 'idea' of India as a unified nation, propagated by Kulkarni is well exemplified in Karnad's plays. In spite of belonging to tradition, the roots playwrights resurrect history as contemporaneity. Karnad in his plays reinterprets the past historical events making them relevant to contemporary times. The corpus of his drama includes the treatment of legendary heroes like Tipu Sultan and Tughlaq, who were among the most dynamic rulers in Indian history. Tipu Sultan's secret aspirations form the substance of the play *The Dreams of Tipu Sultan*. The play takes into account the early attempts of the colonizers to establish their supremacy in India.

Karnad's plays also foreground the way the historians give twisted facts in the name of objectivity. *Tughlaq* depicts "the descent of an over-ambitious Mughal King whose intentions are overshadowed by his own callous demeanour" (Balaram, 4). In the character of Tughlaq Karnad has mirrored the intrigue of the present day politicians as well. Karnad invariably attacks dogmatic approach to religion. *Tughlaq* transcends the limits of historical time by representing the corrupt, unscrupulous and heartless attitude of a callous ruler. Karnad also gives voice to some political issues and suggests corrective measures as in *Taledanda*. In this play he speaks of uprooting the evil of caste discrimination and of ushering into a new era of enlightenment where there will be no darkness. Basavanna's character is an embodiment of the spirit of modernity. Karnad portrays him as a revolutionary figure who raises a voice against those who want to perpetuate caste and class hierarchy. The play is a powerful comment on how power politics operates in our society. It also takes into account the disparities between the upper and lower castes.

When India as a newly independent nation was striving to establish its own identity, the roots playwrights created a perfect ambience, where the idea of a modern nation could be envisioned. The ideas of a unified and united nation are powerfully exemplified through Karnad's historical plays. In *Bali: The Sacrifice* Karnad voices the issue of non-violence and debates at length on the conflict between actual violence and intended violence. The idea of violence is presented through the power structures operating in our society. Karnad incorporates other issues like religion, morality and ideological differences to comment upon the way some regressive practices still hold sway over people's minds.

An analysis of Karnad's plays reveals that his works reflect the pivotal concerns and agendas of the roots movement. Karnad recognizes the theatrical diversity that exists in our country and as noted already, re-defines the modern Indian theatre by the intermingling of traditional genres and western techniques to create an indigenous modern Indian theatre. Karnad's plays embody this aspect of the roots practitioners who used Western theatre as a model but simultaneously made conscious efforts to evolve the Indian performance based genres, giving them a distinctively modern flavour.

Karnad deftly employs the conventions and motifs of folk theatre like masks, curtains, dolls, story within a story to "project a world of intensities, uncertainties and unpredictable denouements" (Sinha, 105). He experiments boldly with this technique and his plays forge a bonding between the past and the present through this as well. He refers to the past while delving deep into the world of myths and folklore. But the spirit of his drama is unmistakably modern. He not only links tradition and modernity but also the grandeur and nobility of the epics like the *Mahabharata* and *Ramayana*, the legacy of legendary heroes, with the simplicity and charm of folk imagination. Thus, mingling the epic, historic and folk strains, his drama acquires a universal appeal and imaginative richness.

Karnad's drama has the tone and expression of great works. His ingenuity and artistic skill consist in the way he examines the tales he incorporates in his drama, from his own point of view along with their social, historical and mythic perspective. He transforms and re-presents a given situation in a unique way, attaching to it an aesthetic value which is the sole aim of drama and theatre per se.

Mahesh Dattani once remarked that without playwrights and directors such as Karnad, Panikkar, and Thiyam, 'we wouldn't have a real modern Indian theatre'. Karnad's drama provided answer to the questions posed by the theatre artists: "What would a modern Indian theatre be? In what ways could theatre be used to reflect and constitute the complex cultures and subjectivities of a newly independent notion?" (Mee, 263) The innovative and vibrant works of Karnad showcase the theories, goals and accomplishments of the theatre of roots movement. Dattani complements playwrights like Karnad who 'have created valuable links between folklore, traditional theatre and the modern Indian audience. They are extremely valuable in creating a modern Indian theatre which is not defined exclusively by urban tastes' (Dattani,Email to Erin . B. Mee)

Works Cited and Consulted

Primary Sources Plays by Girish Karnad

Karnad, Girish. *The Fire and the Rain.* New Delhi: Oxford University Press, 2000.

----. *Yayati.* New Delhi: Oxford University Press, 2008.

----. *Hayavadana.* New Delhi: Oxford University Press, 2000.

----. *Naga-Mandala* (Play with a Cobra). New Delhi: Oxford University Press, 2000.

----. *Tughlaq.* New Delhi: Oxford University Press, 2003.

----. Two Plays by Girish Karnad: *The Dreams of Tipu Sultan* and *Bali: The Sacrifice.*

New Delhi: Oxford University Press, 2005.

----. *Collected Plays*, Vol. 2, *Tale-Danda, The Fire and the Rain, The Dreams of Tipu*

Sultan, Two Monologues: Flowers, Broken Images. New Delhi: Oxford University Press, 2009.

Secondary Sources

(a) Other Books

Abrams, M.H. *A Glossary of Literary Terms.* 3 ed. New Delhi: Machmillan, 1999.

Anand, Mulk Raj. *The Indian Theatre.* New York: Roy Publishers, 1951.

Ashcroft, Bill, et al. *Key Concepts in Post-Colonial Studies.* London: Routledge Publishers, 2004.

Babb, Lawrence. "Glancing: Visual Interaction in Hinduism." *Journal of Anthropological Research*, 37: 387-401, 1981.

Babu, M. Sarat. "Gender Deformity: Tendulkar's Kamala, Karnad's Naga-Mandala and Rakesh's Half-Way House." *Indian Drama Today - A Study in the Theme of Cultural Deformity.* New Delhi: Prestige Books, 1999.

Bhatta, S. Krishna. *Indian English Drama: A Critical Study.* New Delhi: Sterling Publishers, 1987.

Brokington, J.L. *The Sacred Thread: A Short History of Hinduism.* Oxford: Oxford University Press, 1992.

Dass, Veena Noble. "Experiment and Innovation in Modern Indian Drama in Translation: The plays of Mohan Rakesh, Badal Sircar, Vijay Tendulkar and Girish Karnad." *Modern Indian Drama* in English Translation. Hyderabad: Tauras Printers, 1998.

Despande, G.P. "Introduction," *Modern Indian Drama: An Anthology.* Delhi: Sahitya Akademy, 2000.

Devi, Mahasweta. *Mother of 1084.* Trans. Samik Bandyopadhyay. Calcutta: Seagull Books, 1997.

Dharwadker, Aparna Bhargava. "Performance, Meaning and the Materials of Modern Indian Theatre: Interview with Girish Karnad," NTQ 11(44): 355-70.

Dodiya, Jaydipsinh. *The Plays of Girish Karnad: Critical Perspectives*. New Delhi: Prestige Books, 1999.

Eliade, Mircea. "The Myths of the Eternal Return." Trans. Williard R. Trask. Princeton: Princeton University Press, 1974.

Eliade, Mircea. *Myths and Mythical Thought*. England: McGraw Hill Books, 1976.

Frye, Northrop. *Anatomy of Criticism*. Princeton, NJ: Princeton University Press, 1957.

Frye, Northrop. *The Stubborn Structure*. Ithaca, NY: Cornell University Press, 1970.

Flahertly, Wendy O'. Introduction. *Hindu Myths: A Sourcebook*, translated from the Sanskrit. By Flaherty. New Delhi: Penguin Books, 1975.

Gandhi, Shanta. "An Approach to our Traditional Theatre." Sangeet Natak 77/78, 14-16.

Gaonker, Dilip Parameshwar. 'On Alternative Modernities', in Dilip Parameshwar Gaonkar. Ed. Alternative Modernities. Duraham: Dute University Press. 2001.

Goel, Savita. "Folk Theatre Strategies in Hayavadana." *The Plays of Girish Karnad: Critical Perspectives*. Ed. Jaydipsinh Dodiya. New Delhi: Prestige Books, 1999.

Grebstein, Herbert Weisinger, Sheldon Norma. "The Mythopoeic Critic." *Perspectives in Contemporary Criticism.* New York: Harper and Row, 1968.

Guerin, Labor, Morgan, Reesman, Willingham. *A Handbook of Critical Approaches to Literature.* 4 ed. Oxford: Oxford University Press, 1999.

Gupta, Santosh. "Naga-Mandala: A Story of Marriage and Love." *The Plays of Girish Karnad: Critical Perspectives.* Ed. Jay dip Sinh Dodiya. New Delhi: Prestige Books, 1999.

Iyengar, Srinivasa K.R. *Indian English Literature.* Hyderabad: Yugadi Publishers, 2000.

Jacob, George C. "Myth as Fulcrum: Lord Ganesha as Dramatic Presence in Hayavadana." *The Plays of Girish Karnad: Critical Perspectives.* Ed. Jaydipsinh Dodiya. New Delhi: Prestige Books, 1999.

Jenkins, Henry. *Textual Poachers: Television Fans and Participatory Culture.* New York: Routledge, 1992.

Jons Veronica. "Indian Mythology." *Library of the World's Myths and Legends.* England: The Hamlyn Publishing Group Limited, 1983.

Joshi, Kireet. "The Mystic Fire." *The Veda and Indian Culture: An Introductory Essay.* Delhi: Motilal Banarsidass, 2003.

Kar, Prafulla C. *Rethinking Indian English Literature.* Delhi: Pencraft International, 2000.

Karnad, Girish. "Author's Introduction." *Three Plays by Girish Karnad: Naga-Mandala, Hayavadana, Tughlaq*. New Delhi: Oxford University Press, 2998.

Karnad, Girish. "Introduction." *Collected Plays*. Vol. 2. By Aparna Bhargava Dharwadker. New Delhi: Oxford University Press, 2009.

Khilnani, Sunil. *The Idea of India*. New York: Farrar, Straus, Girouse, 1999.

Kirtinath, Kurtkoti. "Introduction." *Hayavadana*. By Girish Karnad. New Delhi: Oxford University Press, 2003.

Kumar, Nand. "Myths in the Plays of Girish Karnad." *Indian English Drama: A Study in Myths*. New Delhi: Sarup and Sons, 2005.

Lidova, Natalia. *Drama and Ritual of Early Hinduism*. Ed. Farley P. Richmond. Delhi: Motilal Banarsidas Publishers, 1994.

Mascario, Juan. *The Bhagvad Gita*. Trans. Noida: Penguin Books India, 1994.

Mee, Erin B. *Drama Contemporary India*. Baltimore, Maryland and London: The Johns Hopkins University Press, 2001.

Mee, Erin B. *Theatre of Roots: Redirecting the Modern Indian Stage*. Calcutta: Seagull Books, 2008.

"Myth." *The Oxford English Dictionary and Thesaurus III*. Oxford: Oxford University Press, 2007.

Naik, M.K. *A History of Indian English Literature.* New Delhi: Sahitya Akademi, 1982.

Naik, M.K. "From the Horse's Mouth: A Study of Hayavadana." *Dimensions of Indian English Literature.* New Delhi: Sterling Publishers, 1984.

Paranjape, Makrand R. "Metamorphosis as Metaphor: Shape-Shifting in Girish Karnad's Play." *New Directions in Indian Drama: With Special Reference to the plays of Vijay Tendulkar, Badal Sircar and Girish Karnad.* Eds. Sudhakar Pandey and Freya Barua. Delhi: Prestige Books, 1994.85.Print.

Pandey, Sudhakar. Freye Tarporemala, eds. *Studies in Contemporary Indian Drama.* New Delhi: Prestige Books, 1990.

Raina, M.K. "Two Approaches to Tradition." *Sangeet Natak,* 77/78: 29-32.

Rangacharya, Adya. *The Indian Theatre.* New Delhi: National Book Trust, 1971.

Rangan, V. "Myth and Romance in Nagamandala or their Subversion." *Girish Karnad"s Plays: Performance and Critical Perspectives.* Ed. Tutun Mukherjee. Delhi: Pencraft International, 2006. 199-207. Print.

Sinha, A.K. "Thematic Concerns and Technical Features." *The Plays of Girish Karnad: Critical Perspectives.* Ed. Jaydipsinh Dodiya. New Delhi: Prestige Books, 1999.

Subiotto, Arrigo. "Epic Theatre: A Theatre for the Scientific Age." *Brecht in Perspective.* Ed. by Graham

Bartram and Anthony Waine. United States of America: Longman Publications, 1982.

Sudhir, Grace. "On the Wings of His Dreams: Re-viewing the Legend and History of Tipu Sultan." *Girish Karnad's Plays: Performance and Critical Perspectives.* Ed. Tutun Mukherjee. Delhi: Pencraft International, 2006.

Taylor, Charles. 'Two Theories of Modernity', in Dilip Parameshwar Gaonkar. Ed. Alternative Modernities. Durham: Dute University Press. 2001.

Vatsyayan, Kapila. *Bharta's The Natyashastra.* New Delhi: Sahitya Akademic, 2003.

Vergese, C. Paul. *Essays on Indian Writing in English.* New Delhi: N.V. Publications, 1975.

Williams, Linda R. *Boomsbury Guides To English Literature: The Twentieth Century From 1900 to the Present Day.*

(b) Articles from the Newspapers

Ahuja, Chaman. "Epic Play." *The Tribune on Sunday.* 8 May, 2005. 8. Print.

Bande, Usha. "Scholar who gave us back our Folklore." *The Tribune on Sunday.* 18 Dec, 2005.4. Print.

Chatterji, Madhushree. "Mission to unravel myths." *The Tribune on Sunday.* 16 Mar. 2008. 5. Print.

Chowdhary, Neelam Mansingh. "Karnad Centrestage." *The Tribune on Sunday.* 9 Apr. 2006. 3. Print.

Dhiman, Kuldeep. "Engaging Vedic Exploration." Rev. of. *Discovering the Vedas: Origins, Mantras, Rituals, Insights, The Tribune on Sunday.* 16 Mar. 2008. 5. Print.

"Invoking Lord Ganesha." *The Times of India.* 27 Aug. 2006. 19. Print.

Kanthwal, Gaurav. "Playful Mischief." *The Tribune on Sunday.* 9 Apr. 2006. 4. Print.

Mahajan, Priyanka. "Ramayana Migrates to Southhall." *The Times of India.* 3 Apr. 2006. 8. Print.

PTI. "Metaphor for a New Age." *The Tribune on Sunday.* 4 Dec. 2005. 7. Print.

Singh, Harbans. "Quest for the Carnal." *The Tribune on Sunday.* 6 Apr. 2008. 4. Print.

(c) Interviews

Allana, Amal. Interview by Amrit Lai. *The Times of India.* 20 Jan. 2007.

Karnad, Girish. Interview by Rajashree Balaram. *Harmony Org Online.* <http://www.harmonyindia.org/hyportal/virtualpageview.jsp?page_id=7483>

Karnad, Girish. Interview. "The World of GSB Konkani: Let me look into the present now - Girish Karnad," 9 Jul. 2005. Web 30 Dec. 2007.

Online Sources

(a) Online Articles on Girish Karnad

Ahuja, Chaman. "Holding a mirror up to Indian Theatre." *Sunday Reading. The Tribune.* 30 May, 1999. Web. 27 Nov. 2006. <http://www.tribuneindia. com>

Asnani, Shyam. "The State of Indian English Drama." *Recent Indian English Literature (A Study since Independence).* Ed. S.D. Sharma. 14 Feb. 2007. Web. 3 Jan. 2008.

Chatterjee, Sudipto. "Speaking of the Play: Hayavadana." <http://www. departmentofdanceanddramahayavadana.html>. 11 Jan. 2005.

Chatterjee, Gautam. "The Return of Karnad." *The Hindu*, Online. 22 Apr. 2005 <http://www.hinduonnet.com/2005/22/04.html>.

Chatterjee, Sandeep. "Seriously Sandeep >> Denigrating Indian Culture: the Girish Karnad way Part I." 26 July, 2006. Web. 7 Oct. 2009.

Chatterjee, Sudipto. "Ratan Thiyam: Elusive Dissent." *Contemporary Indian Theatre An Overview.* Web. 30 Dec. 2007.

Dattani, Mahesh. E-mail to Erin B. Mee. 26 Nov. 2003.

"Folk or Traditional Theatre." Modern Theatre in India: Bengali Theatre. History and Types of Theatre. 26 Mar. 2010 <http://www.culturopedia.com/ theatre/folk_theatre.html>.

Gabula, Abbasali. "Tuglaq at SPJIMR, Mumbai." 12 Jan. 2004. Web. 2 June, 2004.

Gupta, Bharat. "Natyashastra: Chapter 28." 30 Dec. 2007. Web.

"Girish Karnad and other Worthies - Part I, II." Web. 17 May, 2006.

Houston, Letischa Beachy. "Analysis of a Passage from T.S. Eliot's the Waste Land: Scrutinizing Eliot's Delibrate Writing." 15 May, 2007. Web. 10 Jan. 2010.

"Jnampeeta Awards - Girish Karnad." <http://www.virtualbangalore.com/online Bangalore_Arts and Culture_Jnanpeeta Awards_Girish Karnad.html>. 2 May, 2004. Web. 23 July, 2007.

Karnad, Girish - Wikipedia, the free encyclopaedia. 1 Apr. 2010. <http://en.wikipedia.org/wiki/Girish-Karnad>.

Lakshman, Ganesha S. "Agnivarsha is to be released in N.Y. on 3 Aug." 9 July, 2006. Web.

"Life Goes on (2010): ST Soha Ali Khan Girish Karnad. Om P. Promo-Preview-Review-Trailor." *Stromglass Production U.K.* 23 Jan. 2010. Web. 7 Feb., 2010.

Morris, Eaves. *The William Blake Archive*, 4 Jan. 2010. <http:/www.blakearchieve.org/ blake/>.

Mee, Erin B. "Star of India: Master Director Ratan Thiyam Brings An Eye-Filling Saga of Good Versus Evil to America." 3 Apr. 2005. Web. 27 Oct. 2009.

Menon, Paravathi. "The Multi-faceted Playwright." *Frontline Online*. Vol. 16. 30 Jan. 1999. Web. 23 Apr. 2006.

Merchant Rehmat, Kalidas S. "Renaissance Man: The multi-faceted Jnanpith winner has a historic vision but a contemporary voice." 12 Apr. 1999. Web. 1 Nov. 2007.

"Political Film Society - The Fire and the Rain." PFS Film Review. 6 Feb. 2004. <http://www.geocities.com/~polfilms/firerain.html>.

Rangan, V. "Myth and Romance in Naga-Mandala or their Subversion." *Girish Karnad's Plays: Performance and Critical Perspectives*. Ed. Tutun Mukherjee. 14 Jan. 2010. Web.

Rukhaya, M.K. "Identity Crisis in Broken Images." By Girish Karnad. 7 Sep. 2008. Web. 10 Jan. 2010.

Ravindran, Nirmala. "Culture Theatre, Conflict Theory." *India Today Online*. 25 June, 2007. Web. 2 Feb. 2010.

"Rooted in Theatre." *Frontline*. Vol. 23. Issue 15. Jul. 29-Aug. 11. 2006. Web. 1 Nov. 2007.

"Ritual Theatre in India." *Modern Theatre in India: Bengali Theatre, History and Types of Theatre*. 26 Mar. 2010. <http://www.culturopedia.com/theatre / folk_theatre.html>

Science Direct-Thinking Skills and Creativity: From Myth to history and back again. 1 Apr. 2010 <http://www.sciencedirect.com / science? ob = Article URL &_udi=B7 XNB-4MTK 99 G-T&- use...>

Vashistha, Samstha. "Review of Tughlaq by Girish Karnad." 2 June, 2004. Web. 13 Aug. 2007.

Yarrow, Ralph. "Consciousness, Literature and the Arts Archive." Vol. 3. Dec. 2002. Web. 16 May, 2006.

"Zine 5: Review of Tughlaq by Girish Karnad." 2 June, 2004 <http://archieve.zine5.com / boo 12.html>

(b) Online Message from Girish Karnad

Karnad, Girish. "The World Theatre Day Message by Girish Karnad, Playwright." 27 Mar. 2002. Web. 16 Oct. 2004.

(c) Websites Consulted:

http://indianwriting blogsome.somefiowers./2007/03/25 / flowers. 10 Jan. 2010.

http://www.washingtonbanglaradio.com. Life goes on. 23 Jan. 2010. 7 Feb. 2010.

http ://en. wikipedia.org/wiki/Girish_Karnad.

http://www.languageindia.com.dollygeorge

http://www.virtualbangalore.com/online Bangalore-Arts and Culture - Girish Karnad.html

http://archive.zine5.com/bookl2.html

http://www.hinduonnet.com/thehinduonnet.html

http://www.geocities.com/poliflms/firerain.html.

http://www.coolavenues.com/bschools/spjimr-tughlaq.php3

http://www.harmonindia.org/hyportal/Virtual Page View.jsp? page_id=7483.

http ://www. culturopedia. com/Theatre/ritualtheatre.html